# Cicada Summers

# Cicada Summers

JORDAN SMITH GRAFFIS

Palmetto Publishing Group
Charleston, SC

*Cicada Summers*
Copyright © 2018 by Jordan Smith Graffis
All rights reserved

First Edition

Printed in the United States

ISBN-13: 978-1-64111-181-2
ISBN-10: 1-64111-181-X

# Contents

# Prologue

My son, you earned the nickname "Billy Rubin" in your second day of life. Born with jaundice, treatment was needed to lower the levels of bilirubin in your blood. As unflattering as it sounds, bilirubin is the brownish yellow substance found in bile, and high levels of bilirubin can be dangerous for babies (and adults, too). Babies with jaundice actually have a brownish-yellow tint to their skin. When the doctor handed you to me for the first time, you looked like you had a tan, like you had just had a fun-filled day outside in our beloved South Carolina Lowcountry rather than a twenty-seven-hour trip through the birth canal (Yes, twenty-seven hours. You damn near killed me. They certainly didn't tell me that was a possibility in Lamaze class). I thought my little bronzed baby was gorgeous. The next day, though, as we sat in a rocking chair next to the window with the natural sunlight pouring in, I could see you were actually yellow, not tan.

As if the pitiful sight of a sickly baby wasn't bad enough, high levels of bilirubin make babies really cranky. So, as I listened to hours and hours of crying and fussing, I decided to name this alter ego of yours, Billy Rubin. And as you know, it stuck, even after you were no longer a fussy, yellowed newborn.

When I gave birth to you, I was twenty-nine years old and thought I had life pretty much figured out. After all, I had survived those awkward teenage years and stumbled and clawed my way through my twenties.

But I was wrong. I was totally, utterly, insanely wrong.

What you would teach me, especially in your first few years of life, was that I had a lot to learn. Actually, I had a lot to *relearn*. The lessons I experienced as a new mom were actually repeats of ones I thought I'd mastered as a child, like the importance of sharing, how to love unconditionally, and that the future is full of possibility. As cliché as these lessons sound, they are what make children so special. Adults can become burdened by responsibility, consumed by stress, and saturated with negativity, losing that luster they had as children.

I don't want that to be you, my sweet Billy Rubin, which is why, as you prepare to have your own child in just six short months, I've written this book for you. Your child will teach you invaluable lessons, and I hope you take notice. This book is a compilation of the lessons you taught me, and I want to share my knowledge with you. And thank you.

As adults, if we're not careful, the world can beat us down. We stop sharing because we get selfish, we put limitations on who and how we love, and when we think of the future, we're only looking forward to mundane events such as paying off the mortgage.

Of course, as parents, it's our job to teach our children. But what raising children taught me is that I was doing just as much learning as I was educating.

When you were really young, I watched you grasp the true meaning of life, and I noticed my own grasp weakening. I'd routinely think, how can adults regain the carefree, loving, so-excited-you-pee-your-pants outlook on life? True, we can't just ignore the responsibilities or stress-inducers that come with being mature adults, but I wanted to believe there was a way to reconnect with what we should have never let go of in the first place. I wanted to see if I could take those important lessons I learned as a child and apply them to adulthood.

At the beginning of each chapter, I've used examples of your childhood adventures and antics to illustrate what's truly important in life. I've written it in such a way that it'll be like reading a children's book about your own adolescence. I've scrounged up old photos of you to create illustrations and capture that child-like innocence, and then throughout the rest of each chapter, I explain how you, as an adult, may be able to mimic your former ideals and behaviors to rediscover true contentment.

This approach is not meant to insult your intelligence with childhood anecdotes and jovial pictures (but who doesn't love illustrations and a break in the narrative?). Instead, I'm hoping it serves as a literary time machine, catapulting you back to a simpler time filled with best friends who are stuffed with cotton, belly-laughs, and the memory of young Billy Rubin (because we all have a little bilirubin in us).

# One

BILLY RUBIN DANCED THROUGH LIFE WITH SOME SPE-
cial characters—Momma, Daddy, Sissy Bobo (that's the nonsensical nickname he gave his baby sister) and Black-Eyed
Hollie (his dog). But there was another member of his pack
that was perhaps the most memorable of all—his grandfather,
Farfar.

"Farfar" means "father's father" in Danish, and Farfar was
as unique as his moniker.

First of all, once Farfar discovered this word for "grandfather," he never went by his legal name again. He was simply
known as Farfar. When he ordered pizza, he'd tell Dominos to
deliver the pie to "Farfar" at his address. When he introduced
himself to Billy Rubin's teachers at preschool, they met a bald,
bearded man named Farfar with no other explanation.

Billy Rubin thought everything Farfar did was cool. They
had a very special relationship. And even though Momma ini-
tially found Farfar to be a bit strange, she quickly became very
fond of him.

She learned to overlook her father-in-law's common practice
of wearing "jorts" (homemade jean shorts) to formal functions

1

and even embraced the matching "jouch" (a homemade pouch, much like a fanny pack, made out of the discarded jean legs he no longer needed after creating his jorts).

Momma, in fact, had many fond memories of Farfar. One of her favorites was the time she put him in charge of bringing snacks to Billy Rubin's preschool class. He ignored the traditional munchies like raisins and Cheerios and instead opted to bring the tots octopus in a can.

While it took Momma some time to embrace Farfar's eccentricities, Billy needed no time to adjust. The rest of the world may view his Farfar as different, but Billy Rubin thought he was the coolest person on the planet. Billy appreciated his Farfar just the way he was—jouch and all—and would never want to change what made him so special. To Billy, to alter a man like Farfar would be to ruin his true character, and he showed nothing but acceptance for his father's father.

I'VE DECIDED TO MAKE THE FIRST CHAPTER ABOUT ACceptance because I believe it's one of the most important character traits a person can possess...and also one of the hardest to master. Acceptance of others is crucial. And acceptance of oneself is freeing. Living a life that combines both is game-changing.

Our world needs more of it.

Writing a book has been something I've fantasized about for more than half of my life. Long before I decided to write the book for you, I wanted to write it for me. Though I went years without ever knowing the topic or timing, I knew there was a story inside of me that would one day surface.

There's a very good reason that I'm writing the book now, in my later years: One, I needed you and Sissy to provide the majority of subject matter, and two, it was nearly impossible to write anything during the craziness of your childhoods.

Three decades ago, when I first put pen to paper, I tried to do it with you, then a toddler, running around.

Living with a toddler, by the way, is complete lunacy, as indicated by the below journal excerpt. (And I can't wait for you to experience it. Pay back, son).

*I can vacuum the entire house while Billy is sleeping, and he doesn't wake up. I can turn on the TV, and he continues to snooze. Hollie can bark, and Billy's slumber remains unaffected. But as soon as my hand silently picks up a pencil to begin working on my book, he opens his eyes and screams for me.*

*"Mom-o!"*

*When I was pregnant, I pictured my perfect baby boy looking up at me with a perfect, sweet little face and with a soft, innocent voice saying "Momma."*

*Instead, in this moment, I have a red-faced, angry toddler screaming "Mom-o," which sounds much less affectionate and flattering.*

*Something else unflattering: He is riding a poop-covered tricycle, having apparently driven it through dog crap. In the span of two minutes, he gets out of bed, hops on a trike, and plows through the crap. It is all over his little toes and the trike's wheels, and he is continuing to drive around, smearing shit all over the floor. My first thought is to run away. Run far, far away. My second thought is to get rid of the dog. My third thought is to consider this book's completion a crap-shoot.*

*In an attempt to prove myself wrong about the book, I ask Graff to watch our red-faced, angry toddler while I go to the coffee shop to write. The red-faced, angry toddler loves hanging out with his daddy. I love writing in peace. I overhear a conversation taking place at the table beside me. I'm sitting next to a guy who's very clearly on a first date and telling his lady friend what brand of dental floss he uses.*

*At least the poopy trike isn't here.*

And that's as far as I got. Fast-forward two years, and I found myself sitting at the kitchen table trying to write with a newborn in a onesie that reads "Little Sister" staring up at me from her bassinet. The more fitting phrase should be "Little Progress," because that's what I was making on this project.

Now that it's finally finished, here's what I want you to take away from this book: This is a story about miracles—from the small ones that occur every day to the large, jaw-dropping ones.

I didn't live a glamorous life. It's actually been quite ordinary. But it has been blessed. And for reasons unbeknownst to me at the time, I recorded my life in a journal, every single day, from the time I moved out on my own at eighteen. At first, I wrote to vent about my parents, to gush about boyfriends, and to rave about college. But as life went on, and the years literally flew by, I became enchanted every day as I read the many other journal entries from that same day in previous years. It was humbling to see how far I had come or motivating to read that life wasn't quite what I thought it would be. I went from writing about college classes and part-time jobs to finding your daddy and welcoming you and Sissy.

So why should my admittedly ordinary life matter to you? Because I have a story to tell. One that I believe you can relate to. These journal entries have allowed me to see that what I considered to be just insignificant events in life were actually part of a grand plan in motion. There's a plan for you, too. And this book contains lessons I've learned along the way, ones that I hope will help you on your own journey.

I say this is a story about miracles because that's what I consider my life lessons to be. As a Christian, I believe these blessings are a gift from God. Don't worry, I'm not going to get all holier-than-thou on you. I'm not here to judge; after all, acceptance is what this chapter is all about. I'm reminding you about my religious beliefs to explain that this book is about me slowly discovering things about myself and my life that I believe God's always known. I am not perfect. Far from it. But that's okay because that's not what Christianity is about. It's about unconditional, unfathomable, indescribable love. And that kind of love is obtained through acceptance—acceptance of others, acceptance of ourselves, acceptance of God's plan. Throughout my life, I've come to realize that in order to achieve this (or try at least), I needed to learn to live like Jesus did. And as his disciple, I believe my responsibility is to demonstrate His love to mankind through my thoughts, actions, and words.

(Disciple means "student," by the way, which I find completely fitting since I, as a disciple, am constantly learning… and failing tests).

I'm not going to say anything you haven't heard before—I'm saying things you need to hear again.

Even if you choose to have different spiritual beliefs than I do, and you absolutely have that freedom and right, I think this book is still relevant. My hope is that it softens your heart. As human beings, we owe it to ourselves, and to each other, to revisit certain life lessons. Sometimes you have to look backward before you can move forward.

When I found myself moving forward into motherhood, I, six months pregnant with you, decided to write a list of all the things I wanted to make sure that I taught you: how to apologize, how to ride a bike, how to be appreciative, just to name a few. Acceptance was on the list, but it was pretty far down.

When you were two years old, you went to preschool orientation and wanted to share your Play-Doh with a fellow classmate. The kid, though, told you that he wouldn't play with you because you were "weird." You were crushed. I was angry. It was on that day that I decided to instill in you the importance of acceptance. I didn't want you to make someone feel the way that kid made you feel.

It's a lesson that took me decades to finally "get." Because we, as adults, do to others exactly what that kid did to you. We immediately judge someone by what we see that's different on the outside. Your Farfar is the perfect example; I was embarrassed by him for a long time, and I'm ashamed of that now. I can never thank him enough for his love and support (and this life lesson he taught me). To think I could've missed out on getting to know this awesome guy because of our differences is sad. It speaks strongly (and negatively) to my character at the time.

What a world we would live in if we could see people the way children do. As a kid, every time you went to the park, you'd see a kid you'd never met before and say "he's going to be my buddy-friend." To you, everyone had the potential to be your confidant. It didn't matter what color their skin was, what clothes they had on, how they fixed their hair, what they had to say—You wanted to get to know them. I can't take credit for that—that's the beauty of a child's nature.

When you were in preschool, your favorite song was "The More We Get Together." And the lyrics perfectly illustrate how you lived your life:

*The more we get together,*
*Together, together,*
*The more we get together,*
*The happier we'll be.*
*'Cause your friends are my friends,*
*And my friends are your friends.*
*The more we get together,*
*The happier we'll be.*

Sadly, we lose the ability to demonstrate unconditional acceptance as we become adults. Our own insecurities, or our belief that we are somehow superior, cloud our vision and lead to a rush of judgment. I believe acceptance is an instinct we're all born with. It's only after the learned behaviors of hatred and intolerance are instilled in us that our instinct gets overturned. Parents have an obligation to not crush the loving, accepting nature of children. Parents should nurture it. Encourage it. Practice it. And when we mess up, acknowledge it.

For me, part of the reason I've fallen short in the acceptance department is because I let my own expectations get in the way. Sometimes I expect people to behave a certain way or think a certain way, for example. Even if I don't intend to, those expectations can creep into the back of my mind. It can be difficult to let go of expectations, even when I desperately want to. I hope you don't fall into that trap.

The mistakes I've made, the consequences I've endured, the victories I've experienced, the people I've loved…they all make up who am I today. I accept it all. And I've been able to accept it all because I've learned to love it all—the good and the bad. As life progresses, it's a constant, conscious decision to repeat the cycle: love and accept, love and accept, love and accept. And that's my prayer for you—that you embrace the same challenging, beautiful, rewarding rotation and love someone who is Far(far) out of your comfort zone.

# Two

Billy Rubin, with his navy-blue eyes and perfectly styled blonde combover, had many talents. Truly, he was as skilled as he was good-looking. He could sing louder than anyone Momma had ever heard (You haven't lived until you've heard "Frere Jacques" on repeat at 103 decibels); he had the awesome ability to apply feelings to inanimate objects (Did you know Christmas trees get sad if you don't turn their lights on?); and he could come up with an elaborate fib and convincingly sell it in under three seconds (A pterodactyl flew in the window and ate Momma's freshly-baked pie, not Billy). What a skill set, indeed.

But one area where Billy could use a little work was communication. He was long-winded and spoke in exciting, animated paragraphs, but Momma and Daddy could only understand a few words. He would end his story, eagerly looking up at them, awaiting a response, but they could only stare down at him with bewilderment on their faces. It was like he was speaking a totally different language. Heck, his dog's real name wasn't even Hollie; it was Hollis. It was a male dog, not female, as the name "Hollie" would suggest. But Billy Rubin couldn't say "Hollis," so over time, the rough-and-tumble, tough-as-nails Jack Russell Terrier succumbed to his new name.

Billy Rubin started going to speech therapy, and Momma thought he was making great progress. Until he went to his preschool's holiday party.

At the gathering, Billy saw his friend Ruby standing with her parents. Billy Rubin, in his red Santa Clause sweater, complete with a furry beard and mustache, confidently walked up to Ruby and her family and said, "Hi, Boobie." Her daddy didn't look too pleased.

Momma continued to work with Billy on his words. Slowly, he began to say "orange" instead of "orgy" (which was a relief to Momma). He also started saying "Brody" when referring to his friend instead of saying "bloated." When talking about his favorite sea creature at the aquarium, the octopus, he no longer said "octopiss." And when he dressed as Frankenstein for Halloween, he no longer said "Frankenstyle." All great progress.

Momma considered each corrected word a small victory (Even though it took Billy *years* to correctly say "firetruck." He would replace the *T* and *R* in "truck" with an *F*. Fire*uck. Really?! Momma thought, *Do you know how embarrassing it is to have your son repeatedly yell that word in front of your pastor as you're all watching a parade?*).

But Billy Rubin made no apologies. He kept working on his words with Momma, and going to speech therapy once a week, but he was perfectly content to speak his own language. His speech did improve, but he never quite lost all of the unique verbal characteristics that made him Billy Rubin. After all, this world is filled with many different languages, all beautiful and interesting. How boring would it be if we all sounded the same? To Billy Rubin, with his navy-blue eyes and perfect blonde combover, acquiring his own language was just another talent to add to his skill set.

I REMEMBER PRAYING FOR THE DAY THAT YOU COULD speak more clearly, and when that day finally came, I missed the funny things you used to say. In the mornings, when you'd correctly ask for "milk" instead of "bilk," my heart hurt a little because it was yet another sign that my little boy was growing up.

Your daddy always said he was excited for you and your sister to grow up. Not in a these-kids-are-driving-me-crazy kind of way. But more like a when-will-they-be-able-to-wipe-their-own-butts kind of way. Totally understandable. I felt that way, too. I certainly didn't want to wish away the time, but there was something magical about the thought of it being just your dad and me again, free from the daily constraints of someone being completely dependent on us (and our butt-wiping abilities).

When you were a child, watching you embrace the different communication of others made my heart happy. Children, in general, are very accepting of differences. Some of your friends had issues with their speech, similar to yours, and you never corrected them. You thought everything they said made perfect sense; you supported their ideas and encouraged them to keep talking.

I used to take you and Sissy to story time at Timrod Library. Remember that? That century-old brick building with the white columns on the big front porch? I loved its tall windows. It was a place where I was always at my happiest, with all the sunlight pouring in, illuminating the dust on the old wood floors. I enjoyed walking through that beautiful library, which smelled like old books, and watching you and Sissy listen with excitement to the stories Mrs. Anna read. You had two friends at story time who routinely mispronounced your real name. Instead of calling you Smith, one friend called you "Sniff," and the other friend called you "Spiffy" instead of "Smitty." I always noticed that their pronunciations threw you off for a second, but you never corrected them, only smiled and engaged. This encounter reminds me that we, as adults, could live a life of peace if we learned to mimic that behavior. Before rushing to correct someone, or invaliding them because they have something unique to say, we should embrace a different voice.

Your daddy and I always hoped you'd continue to embrace different ideals as you got older, for many reasons, but mainly because we knew you'd probably one day find a life partner, and commitment to that person is all about accepting dissimilarities.

Graff and I got married on a plantation in Charleston. The huge, white Georgian-style home was built in the late 1700s and overlooks the Ashley River. We said our self-written vows on the front lawn. Your dad promised to tell me every single day how much I meant to him (he kept his promise). I vowed to talk less, listen more, and learn to be a better cook (I didn't keep the latter promise, and I constantly struggled to honor the other two).

The dance floor was on the bank of the Ashley. Lanterns hung from white ribbons in the trees, blowing in the warm October night air. Everyone I've ever loved was there, either physically or spiritually. The last song we danced to before hopping into the back of a white, vintage Rolls Royce and speeding away was Van Morrison's "Into the Mystic."

The very first line is my favorite: *We were born before the wind.*

I once asked your dad what he thought the line "born before the wind" meant. His response was a prime example of how men and women speak different languages.

My interpretation of the line: We, Graff and I, started before the wind. Meaning, it was just us before the chaos; kids, jobs, and bills can all feel like getting sucked up into a tornado at times. Our marriage started with just us and will end with just us, long after the wind dies down.

Your dad's interpretation of the line: He didn't have one. He reasoned that the line didn't make sense because there has always been tornadoes and hurricanes, so wind has always been "a thing." He thought Van Morrison was likely three sheets to the wind when he wrote that line.

I mean, come *on*...could we be any further off?!

I don't want to give you the wrong impression of your dad and I, though. Yes, we, like most couples, have always been very opposite in a lot of ways. Therefore, we communicate very differently. But most of the time, despite our differences, we've moved forward in sync. Early in our marriage, I used to get really frustrated with how differently we communicated, worrying we may never be on the same page which oftentimes caused me to feel alone. But in a marriage, you have the choice to either grow apart or grow together. And growing together involves realizing two people can mean the same thing by saying it two different ways. In your own marriage, when you undoubtedly find yourself saying two different things and meaning two different things, though, like your dad and I did with the "Into the Mystic" interpretation, it's important to realize that's okay, too. Embracing individual concepts and ideas is crucial for a strong union.

When I met your dad, we were twenty years old and at a party in Knoxville, Tennessee. I was in town visiting friends who attended the University of Tennessee, and as fate would have it, Graff, who was a student there, knew my friends. We met at their get-together.

I quickly realized how different we were. He was shy, and I was outgoing; he was a realist, and I was a dreamer; he was certain long-distance relationships didn't work, and I was willing to give us a chance.

It was the only time in my life that I was meeting someone for the first time but felt like we were already connected (other than my own children), as cliché as that sounds. It felt like not knowing your dad wasn't an option.

Despite ourselves, your dad and I were brought together and would remain together. Years later, we would say how much differently our lives would be if I hadn't driven to Knoxville that weekend or if he had decided to go to a different party. But I always knew that wasn't possible. Fate wouldn't allow us to miss each other.

His blonde hair was buzzed; his light-blue eyes saw right through me; and his soul was the most genuine of anyone I'd ever met. That night at the party, I thought he was attentive and honest and witty and sharp. And to this day, those are still the qualities that draw me to him.

We sat by a camp fire, and I could see my breath in the November air. I was shivering, but I didn't want to go inside. I needed to know him. He told me about his parents' recent divorce and how much that hurt him. He said your Gigi and Farfar had known for a long time that their relationship wasn't working, but they waited until your dad, the youngest child, went away to college before they separated because they thought it would be easier for their kids to understand if they were older. I admired how selfless that sounded and remember thinking I hoped I could meet your grandparents.

Thinking back on that story about Gigi and Farfar, it's an example of the beauty that comes from accepting different languages. They weren't saying, or wanting, the same things in life, but they were determined to respect each other by remaining friends even though they couldn't remain spouses. Divorce often creates very different results. It's special when two people can accept their differences and part amicably for the sake of those who love them. They both realized being bitter solved nothing, as is the case with every single situation in life.

While your dad and I have our differences, the older we get, the more I realize how alike we truly are. And one thing we've always agreed on is that while Knoxville was where we met, our love story began on Saint Simons Island in Georgia, and that is where it will end (we want to retire there).

Graff moved to the island after graduating from college, and I spent a lot of time there, visiting.

Mallery Street is the main drag on the Island. Many Saturday mornings, we'd wander through the eclectic shops. In the afternoon, we'd grab a burger and a root beer float at Zuzu's Diner; and our evenings were spent on the pier, watching the sunset.

The first time I visited Graff, it was a cicada summer. A cicada summer is one in which millions of cicadas—red-eyed, winged locusts—emerge from the soil after living in tunnels underground for more than a decade at a time. They then climb the nearest tree and shed their shells.

The sound of cicadas is unforgettable. The male cicadas make a very distinct screaming noise as they search for mates, and the summer air is filled with their droning song. During a cicada summer, trees from the Carolinas to New England are humming with millions of these insects. Cicadas invade different states during different years, depending on the species. So early in my life, as I moved to various states along the East Coast, the cicadas always seemed to find me. When I'd hear the first hums of a cicada summer, I'd know it was going to be a season to remember.

Every cicada summer I've experienced has had a profound impact on my life. They are seasons in my life where I've re-emerged, either because I've come out of my old shell or because I'm leaving a dark place searching for the light. In addition to these reasons, during my St. Simons cicada summer, I, like the locusts, was searching for a mate.

On the island, the smell of pluff mud from the marsh land always hangs in the thick, humid air, and the beautiful sight of the Atlantic Ocean can be seen from many vantage points. My favorite was the gazebo next to the St. Simons Lighthouse on the southern tip of the island. The black and white structure was built in 1810, and the lighthouse keeper's brick cottage is still standing next to the landmark. Both are truly beautiful and, to this day, bring peace to my soul.

During that first visit to the island, I sat at the gazebo, alone, for hours one day, thinking. I had just received my master's degree from Columbia University, but felt like a master of nothing. I had far more questions about life than answers.

*Sitting on this wooden bench has been one of the best times in my life. The waves are crashing, and the gazebo is beautiful, and the wind is loud, and I feel so small. The world feels so big...so engulfing around me...but instead of being scared, I want to embrace it.*

*I can't imagine where I'm going to end up. I can't imagine having a successful job interview and landing a gig and loving it and living alone and establishing my own life.*

*I wish I remember what it was like to learn to walk. I can't imagine how frustrating it would be, when all you really want to do is run, but you can't even walk.*

*I feel like I'm learning to walk again. But what I really want to do is take off in a dead sprint.*

*I love this island. If I lived here, I would come to write at the gazebo every day. I love that pier, the one with the steps that just disappear into the water when the tide is high. I've been thinking a lot. I'm at such an unusual place in my life. And I'm not sure if I will look back on this experience and be glad that it is over or miss this time in my life. The hair on my arms is sticking straight up. There's electricity in my excitement and in the air—a storm is brewing off the coast, much like the one churning inside of me.*

*A big part of me, the unrealistic, crazy part, really loves the idea of just scrapping my life plans and creating new ones. How about staying on St. Simons for the rest of the summer while I figure everything out? Staring out over the waves, it seems feasible. I feel so alive and so creative here.*

Your dad and I returned to the island five years later, shortly after we got married. Still feeling creative, I had the corny idea of putting a message in a bottle and throwing it off of my beloved Mallery Street pier. The message was a poem I wrote him for his twenty-eighth birthday. We had only been married six months. Life was exciting and new, and we retreated back to a place that felt familiar to us for that birthday weekend getaway.

We put our poem into the bottle (a champagne bottle that our realtor gave us when we closed on our first house) and tossed it into the Atlantic.

Throwing the bottle wasn't the romantic moment I had envisioned, though. First of all, I was convinced that we were going to get arrested for littering, so I made Graff wait for hours in our car until I was sure no one was on the pier to see what we were doing.

When we were finally alone on the pier, I then began to worry about that isolation. I was convinced we were going to get mugged. (In truth, no one is awake on St. Simons Island at two in the morning. No one. Not even the muggers. It's a sleepy little town, as dreamy as the southern drawl spoken by the islanders).

When Graff launched the bottle from the pier, it made the loudest thudding splash I've ever heard. (Looking back, I probably didn't choose the best bottle. It had heavy silver embellishments on it. I should have kept it, really. It was too pretty to throw into the ocean. But it was sentimental, and so was I).

That's my fondest memory of the island. I still get that anxious feeling in my gut when I think about the fear and excitement of that night. Fear and excitement are easily lost in a marriage, despite their importance. The everyday-ness of life can make a marriage mundane, but vivid emotions make a relationship real. And worth holding on to.

And that's my prayer for you—that your life's partner always pushes you out of your comfort zone and always loves you despite your communication differences. The goal isn't necessarily to make life easy, but to make it worth living.

I pray you two ride off into the sunset (or watch the sun set from the Mallery Street pier).

# Three

By the time Billy Rubin was sixteen months old, he had already mastered many important life skills: sitting up, standing, crawling, blowing spit bubbles, and finding the most inopportune time to vomit in public.

But it was the day he took his first steps that seemed like the biggest milestone to Momma. Billy didn't just take one or two steps; he started running and never stopped. It signified the day he transitioned from a baby to a toddler.

Before he started walking, Momma would take Billy Rubin on peer play dates so he could learn to interact with kids his own age. All of those kids, though, were already walking, even the ones far younger than Billy. Their parents cautioned Momma that something might be physically wrong with Billy, and Momma worried. The main cause for concern was that Billy never even *tried* to walk; he was perfectly content with crawling and not exploring something new.

On a cold January evening, as Billy Rubin crawled around on the living room floor, he pulled himself up on the coffee table and saw Momma's empty 16-ounce plastic water bottle. His eyes lit up. A look of determination washed over him. Billy stuck the water bottle in his mouth, held his arms out to the side, and took off running.

To this day, Momma isn't sure why the water bottle triggered Billy's desire to run, but it was the funniest sight, watching Billy Rubin, wearing just a diaper, the water bottle protruding out like a duck's bill, and Billy's two chubby arms straight out like the wings of an airplane.

She knew this might be bad parenting, to let a kid run around with a water bottle in his mouth, for fear that he could fall and jam the bottle down his throat. But she was afraid if she took the bottle away, he wouldn't be able to run. She decided to roll the dice.

Sure enough, though, he fell. There was no need to go to the emergency room to have the bottle extracted from his esophagus, but it still wasn't a pleasant situation. There was the crumpled water bottle lying helplessly on the kitchen floor, much like Billy Rubin's determination and confidence, and Momma feared this would deter Billy from trying again. How do you explain to a toddler that falling down is just a part of life?

Turns out, she didn't need to. Billy Rubin mastered this lesson all on his own. Determined to not be intimidated by something new, he picked himself back up, inserted the crinkled water bottle, and took off once again. And as Billy got older, this is how he continued to live his life, undeterred by the speedbumps, at his own pace, and on his own path determining his own method to success. Somehow, he knew that not everyone learned to walk one step at a time.

I REMEMBER HOW TIMID YOU WERE WHEN IT CAME TO the new experience of walking. It seemed like I could almost see your internal debate as your wobbly legs where braced for a step but your chubby little hand wouldn't let go of the couch— your body wanted to move, but your brain was hesitant.

Similar to accepting other languages is the idea of not being afraid of things—people, situations, experiences—that are new to us or that we do not understand. This fear prevents evolution and understanding, and I am guilty of it. I tend to want to live in my comfortable, predictable bubble and not stray too far from what feels familiar and safe.

When you were a baby, I was holding you during a church service one Sunday when I heard two prophetic phrases in what would become one life-changing sermon for me: *Fear is the enemy of faith* and *Failure is not fatal*.

If you've not heard those before, let them sink in.

As I've already told you, I believe God has a plan for my life, and He's often called me to places that are uncomfortable or for reasons that I do not understand. My job as a Christian has always been to follow. But oftentimes, my initial reaction was to recoil. And there have been times, I'm ashamed to admit, that I haven't been obedient. I chose to ignore the calling because I was afraid. But once I heard the words "fear is the enemy of faith," I became much more aware of my trust in God and His plan. Saying you trust God and showing you trust God are two different things. I have chosen to walk by faith instead of sight, even when I'm scared to move. This brings me to my next point: "Failure is not fatal." So what if I fall down? I can always get back up. It's no secret that sometimes the best lessons are learned while you're stumbling, and faith is strengthened when we see that we not only survived, but can keep moving.

Speaking of moving, as you know, I grew up in Kenova (West Virginia's best kept secret). I love my hometown, but I spent much of my childhood daydreaming about a total life change: moving to New York City. I finally got my chance when I was accepted to Columbia University for graduate school. But when it came time to bid farewell to West Virginia, it was one of the more gut-wrenching experiences of my life.

Kenova. Most people have never heard of it, but I'm so glad you have.

When I was growing up, Kenova's claim to fame was the Pumpkin House, where every Halloween, the homeowner put over three thousand jack-o-lanterns, a number that rivaled Kenova's population, on every peak, roof, and porch of the old Victorian. It was original and memorable, and I'd like to think Kenova is, too.

I love that small town, sitting on the borders of Kentucky and Ohio, which is how it got its name: K-E-N for Kentucky, O for Ohio, and V-A for (West) Virginia.

The town still has quaint, tree-lined streets. In fact, every street is named after a tree. It has a century-old drug store (complete with a soda shop) on Chestnut Street; a two-story brick elementary school on Poplar (where I attended, as well as my parents and grandparents); and a meticulously groomed baseball field on Oak (where I sat the bench during softball playoffs in eighth grade. Sports were never my thing).

When I moved to New York, I'd never even seen a subway, let alone ridden on one. I was intimidated by all the honking cars, and I'd never seen people walk so fast.

(I'm not trying to equate my experience to genuinely terrifying encounters. People face unimaginable horrors every single day, all over the world, and I am, in no way, trying to compare my story. I was at Columbia to earn a degree in journalism, and I was always told to "report what you know." So, this is what I know).

This journal entry sums up my fear of the unknown, and my desperation to hold on to the familiar, better than my recollection ever could:

*I'm anxious…so, so anxious…to start school. I just want to get it over with. The majority of my fear comes from the unknown. I just don't know what to expect, so it scares me. I'm scared to meet people, but I'm also scared of not knowing anyone. I'm not ready. I want to hit the pause button until I can gather myself. I keep thinking that I'll go to my first day of school, walk into the admissions office to get my class schedule, and find out they accepted me by mistake. I actually have a back-up plan for if that happens: I'll ride the subway back downtown, grab a slice of pizza from Carmine's, and flip NYC the bird…er, I mean flash NYC a peace sign…and blow it a kiss goodbye.*

I didn't end up having to kiss New York goodbye (at least not without graduating from Columbia first). I stuck it out, but it wasn't a pretty sight.

I immediately felt as though I didn't quite fit in to the Ivy League, big-city crowd. The first time I met my classmates was at a back-to-school picnic. I brought Lays potato chips and a two-liter of Coca-Cola to share. I immediately felt judged by the girls who brought organic fruit. (It was the first time I realized organic fruit existed). I felt judgment again when asked what I thought of the required summer readings (I didn't have much to contribute to the conversation because I didn't know there were required summer readings). I should also mention that I brought Black-Eyed Hollie, then a puppy, to the picnic, and while seated in a "conversation circle" discussing those summer assignments, Hollie hunched over and had a bout of diarrhea right in the middle of the group. But the ultimate judgment came from a guy who would later become a class officer. When answering his question about where I was from, his response was, "Oh, that's so sad. All of that poverty in the coal counties. I'm so sorry you're from there." Furthermore, for the entire year, I was known as "the girl with the accent." My class consisted of people from all around the world. For many students, English was their second language. Yet I was known as the girl who spoke differently. Throughout my time at Columbia, I was embarrassed by my Appalachian twang.

*It's the night before school starts. I feel vulnerable, scared, unsure.*

*I want to think I can conquer this. If this was the night before my first day of school in undergrad, I'd probably stay up late taking shots and playing darts at the Union to celebrate a new school year at Marshall. But this is Columbia. I need an Ivy League amount of sleep or something.*

*One thing that really bothers me (and I hope that I can read this entry ten months from now when I'm receiving my diploma and realize that I was worried for nothing) is that I'm not a typical Columbia student. I don't look the same; I don't sound the same; I don't dress the same; I'm not educated the same. I'm not like the rest of them. I've never lived outside of Kenova. Most of these people are from outside of the country, or they have at least been out of the country at some point. I don't even have a passport. They have at least one master's degree already. They're more educated, more worldly, older, have career experience…and I don't mean to sound like the queen of her own pity party, but gee whiz…I can't help but feel intimidated. This is a scary thing. Right now, at 8:46 the night before school starts, I'd honestly rather run away, to anywhere, than wake up tomorrow and go to Columbia. I know I've been given a gift, and I swear I don't mean to sound ungrateful. I'm just scared. And I feel really alone. I have no friends or family here. I spend my days holed up in this closet-sized apartment with Hollie, the diarrhea-riddled canine. I'm tugged by the fear of wearing the wrong outfit tomorrow or the other kids not liking me or having to do an insane amount of work that's too hard or not being smart enough. But the thing that honestly scares the absolute crap out of me is letting myself down. I'm terrified of screwing this up. I have been given a gift. I have. I have. I have. And I can't mess this up. I'm so afraid of this getting taken away from me. I just want to be proud of myself in the end and know that I did everything I could to live in the moment and take advantage of the opportunity. I want to come out of this without regrets and with a promising future. A lot of people are proud of me, and I don't want to let anyone down. I hope I can look back on this entry the way I've done with other old entries lately. I want to be in a better place, even if better only means wiser.*

Kenova had one grocery store, nearly a dozen churches, and countless characters.

My grandmother was one of the characters. I wish you could've met her. A former nurse, "Mamaw Eleanor," as I called her, was nurturing and kind-hearted, and when I was a kid, she was always reminding me to wear my coat and eat a cheese sandwich and "hug her neck." She slipped me five-dollar bills when no one was watching, and she taught me how to ride my bike. To this day, I've never seen a sixty-year-old woman run as fast as she did as she held on to my handle bars, trying to get me started.

Mamaw dyed her hair blonde, refusing to succumb to the gray, and she always had her nails painted mauve. She never missed a Sunday in church or a Monday watching me in ballet class. In my eyes, she was perfect. A true southern lady.

But that's not to say she was uptight. She did teach me a lot about the Bible, but she also taught me what it meant to "take a dump," as in: "Oh my word, the neighbor's cat is taking a dump on my begonias."

I spent a lot of time at her house in the summers while my parents worked, so I can't think of a cicada summer without thinking of her. Throughout my first cicada summer, my younger brother and I played kick-the-can with our neighbors at precisely 9 p.m. every single night as the cicadas serenaded us. The can was on my driveway, but I never kicked it because one of the opposing team members, the can guard, was more than six feet tall in the sixth grade. I didn't stand a chance against him. Always petite, I weighed sixty pounds and could sit inside my saxophone case. But that summer made me incredibly happy and still makes me smile to this day when I think about how safe I felt, as all children should feel, during that time. My only concern back then was kicking a can and winning a game.

My cicada summer as a teenager was the first time my world didn't feel safe. Mamaw was diagnosed with breast cancer. She handled it with grace, though. True to character, she dressed up for every chemo appointment. She wore numerous gold bracelets on her thin, fragile wrists and a blonde wig on her bald head as my grandfather pushed her in a wheelchair into the hospital each week.

But the light in her eyes started to dim, and my outlook did as well. I didn't understand how something so ugly could happen to a soul so beautiful.

There's no way to accurately describe the physical and mental effects of cancer on both the patient and the family. I will never forget the feeling of utter helplessness and hopelessness as I watched Mamaw battle it.

And battle it, she did. She still insisted on making her famous green beans and fried chicken for Christmas dinner and still went to church every Sunday. She could no longer walk to the alter for communion, so I took communion with her in the pew. That set the tone for the next several years—adjusting to a new normal.

During this time, Mamaw began collecting angel figurines. She'd get them from the hospital gift shop, the church bazaar, yard sales. Friends would give them as gifts. My grandfather soon had to build shelves throughout their house to display all of them. Looking back, I think I now understand why she wanted to surround herself with these angels—she knew she would soon be one.

I was with her in the hospital when she passed away. I was twenty-one. She had gone into remission once, but a few years later, the cancer returned. I was so unbelievably close to her that sometimes I wonder if I would've had the courage to leave Kenova if she was still there. I think my departure would've broken her heart, and she was someone I always wanted to make smile. There are still days, decades later, that when something really good happens to me, or something really bad happens, my first thought is to call Mamaw. And each time, it's a gut-wrenching realization when I can't pick up the phone and hear her voice.

Her death was profound for me, not just because I lost my grandmother but also because I lost my "safe person." Do you have a safe person? Maybe I'm the only one. My definition of a safe person is someone you can't imagine life without, someone you know would do anything for you, someone you can always count on, someone who makes you feel protected and comforted at all times. She became my safe person when I was in elementary school. She was spending the night at my house while my parents were out of town. When she kissed me goodnight, I asked her to stay in my room because I was afraid of the dark. But she told me if she stayed, I wouldn't go to sleep, so she promised to instead sit outside of my room, at the bottom of the stairs, until I fell asleep. I waited for what felt like a long time, alone in the darkness, wanting to sneak out and catch Mamaw not on the stairs. But when I peeked out of my bedroom door, she was still sitting there. Watching. Protecting. Loving.

As a mother, I always found myself watching, protecting, and loving because I realized how important it was to make my children feel safe. You and Sissy deserved it. And what I got in return is the ability to watch my children blossom into adults who can conquer their fears.

Growing up, there wasn't much you were afraid of. You had the confidence of a child, which is hard to describe and nearly impossible to emulate. In fact, you were so sure of yourself that oftentimes it served as a reminder to me to keep moving forward in life. You had the motivation to try new things and the security of knowing I would be behind you no matter what. And if you were afraid, or if you did fall down, you had the valuable skill of being able to bounce back quickly and move on to the next item on the agenda. You didn't stay down for long. That can be hard for adults to do. Even now, I tend to wallow in fears or failures and spend too much time licking my wounds.

Without my safe person in New York, I wondered if I'd be able to navigate this new life by myself. But God always provides. It was a turning point for me—to be completely out of my comfort zone, stripped of everything I ever knew, and to trust despite my fear. To renew my faith. To evolve. To soar through an experience that could've very easily grounded me. Looking back, I realize that sometimes you have to be torn down to be able to grow stronger.

I spent the summer after graduating from Columbia living in my childhood bedroom at your Gris and Nona's house while I searched for a job. My parents were there to support and encourage me, just as they always had, but I realized that at this weird crossroads in my life, I had to learn how to plot my own course.

I poured my heart out in my journal each night, proud of my recent accomplishments, but terrified of the unknown and scared of the next calling. Looking back, I was writing about my current one.

*The air outside smells like kick-the-can. And the cicadas are as loud as I've ever heard them. Whenever I write my book, I'm going to call it Cicada Summers, because just like with my previous cicada summers, the hair on my arms is standing up. I know my life is about to transform. I don't know when, and I don't know how, but I know the change is coming. Just like with my book—it's coming.*

*And while these words seem incredibly optimistic and positive, it couldn't be further from how I feel. Everyone else is moving forward in their lives. And then here I am, back to my eleven-year-old summer, doing chores for Mom and hiding out in my room all day and going to bed early at night because I still have no friends. I feel like I've learned so much since I was eleven, but how much has really changed?*

*I think I'm being forced to relive some of my childhood before I completely transition into adulthood. And it seems so unfair. But, I still have faith; I still believe there's light at the end of the tunnel. I pray that one day I look back on this entry and feel safe again.*

Trusting and following God doesn't mean you won't hit turbulence. This life was not created to be free of pain, fear, sadness, and frustration. After all, there was pain in the offering. When I think about how God gave His only son, Jesus, and sent him to die for our sins so that we may have eternal life, it's almost impossible to imagine that kind of love. As a mother, I look at you and Sissy, and the thought of you dying, let alone *knowing* you were put on this earth to die on a cross the way Jesus did, stops my breath. Truly. I can't even type that sentence without tears streaming down my face. To give my children to save the lives of people I don't even know? Unfathomable. It's too much to fully process. *That* is unconditional love. How can I not follow someone who loves me that much? And knowing how much he loves me makes the darkness of uncertainty tolerable.

My prayer for you is that you that if you feel called, you go; if you feel scared, you walk; if you feel doubt, you pray. Most of all, I hope you'll find that if you peek through the darkness, you'll see that your safe person is still there, and you are not alone.

# Four

When Momma worked, she couldn't wait to come home and hear how Billy Rubin's and Sissy Bobo's days had been.

Farfar babysat them while Momma was at the office, and while it's true that they always had a fun adventure with their grandfather, Billy's recollection of the day's events was always a bit outlandish.

"What did you do today, Billy?" Momma asked.

"I went on an adventure with a mountain goat and ate a jellyfish and drove Farfar's car to the grocery store! I bought some bubble bath because the goat was stinky," exclaimed Billy.

"You ate a jellyfish?" questioned Momma.

"No."

"You could reach Farfar's gas pedal and brake all by yourself?"

"No."

"You bathed a goat?"

"No."

"So, you told a big fib?"

"I wasn't fibbing! I was story-telling!"

It took Billy years to realize when and how to appropriately insert a story into dialogue. Momma repeated over and over that he must tell the truth when being asked a question. She was sure he'd become known as the boy who cried jellyfish since his narratives never turned out to be true. But eventually, Billy caught on, and during story time, unlike most children who read narratives from books, Billy always told his own colorful, inventive, unforgettable story, and they usually involved a mountain goat.

You get your story-telling abilities from me (and that's not always a good thing). I'm just a sucker for interesting tales. I'd love when you'd stand on the fireplace hearth, speak into a fly swatter like a microphone and prepare to tell a big tale: "Ladies and instruments, boys and squirrels, I have a story for you...."

I always wanted you to be brave—brave enough to try new things, brave enough to trust your instincts and abilities, and as you'll read about in this chapter, brave enough to create your own story.

My love of story-telling is why I thought going into the journalism field was a good idea. I wanted to tell other people's stories. What I quickly realized, though, was that line of work would give me a lot of my own to tell.

My first full-time job was at the ABC affiliate in Gainesville, Florida where I was a journalist.

I earned my bachelor's degree in broadcast journalism from Marshall University in West Virginia (Go, Herd!) before attending Columbia, and I had big intentions of hitting the ground running and changing the world through my reporting. I figured I'd contribute to society by writing award-winning stories about consumer reports, politics, and crime.

And indeed, my first assignment was an in-depth, investigative piece.

But it wasn't quite the earth-shattering, life-changing subject matter I was hoping for. My assignment: Spend the night in the middle of the Ocala National Forest, in a centuries-old "ghost town," to see if it was haunted.

*Right. . . .*

So a colleague and I loaded our equipment and sleeping bags into the back of a fourteen-year-old news van with more than 250,000 miles on it, and prayed it would make the hour-long drive from Gainesville to Ocala.

We arrived as the sun was setting. I turned off the main highway onto a bumpy, dirt road and entered the forest. It felt like we drove for miles past countless live oak trees until we reached a house. The owner of the ghost town, which was named Kerr City, was a descendant of one of the founders. He lived on the property, and had allowed us to stay in one of the original cabins.

Kerr City was established in the 1880s and had a hundred residents at its peak. The town had a hotel, sawmill, general store, pharmacy, post office, and a church that also served as a school. Kerr City was a stage coach stop for travelers commuting to Ocala. It became a thriving citrus town but was deserted after a freeze in 1894 wiped out the crops.

When I visited, there were fourteen buildings remaining, including the post office, a Texaco Station (apparently the oldest working one in Florida at the time), and some cabins.

I don't remember much from that night, as I have tried to block it from my memory, but there are bits and pieces that still haunt me: the howling noises the wind made as it whipped through the old, brick fireplace; the sight of an antique porcelain doll, resting against a pillow in one of the bedrooms, its glass eyes illuminating as the camera light swept over them; and the sound of clawing against the front door.

I'm not joking. This is not a Billy Rubin-style "fib."

The clawing wasn't made by a ghost, though. Worse—it was a bear.

So, my coworker and I made a beeline out the backdoor to our news van and spent the entire night trying to sleep in the front seats. I remember reclining the driver's seat back as far as it would go so I couldn't see out the windshield. I didn't know what I was more afraid of—seeing the figure of a long-dead citrus farmer staring back at me in the total blackness…or a hungry bear.

And if I thought that ridiculous story was just my assignment editor's way of breaking in the new kid, I was wrong. I would go on to do many more equally goofy stories. One time, my producer insisted I hold a baby alligator during a live shot. It turned out to be one of the more embarrassing moments of my life when the alligator blew snot all over my blouse on live TV. During another live shot, for a story about a local ice-skater going to the Olympics, my producer insisted I lace up some skates and hit the ice…and that's literally what I did. Not only did I fall down, but I couldn't get back up. I had to do the entire report while sitting on my wet, sore butt (and equally bruised ego).

But my time in Gainesville was life-changing, in a good way. Yes, I would fall down, but more often than not, I would learn to fly (I never did learn to ice-skate, though). I discovered so much about myself and what I'm capable of during my two years there. I learned that in this life, your story can take you to some amazing places, teach you invaluable lessons, and fill holes in your life that you never knew existed. I met my two closest friends while working in Gainesville and my love for them carried with me long after I moved away. The best stories, in my opinion, are the ones in which the ending is unpredictable.

That's truly the greatest thing about my time in news—it was unpredictable and so was its ending.

After working in the journalism field for six years, I decided to walk away. I desperately wanted children and also a career that was more conducive to family life.

Of course, that meant I'd never become a network news anchor like I hoped when I was a kid. And through the wisdom that comes from age and life experience, I've learned that it's okay, and sometimes necessary, to change your dreams. It's perfectly acceptable to chase new ambitions. It's not a failure. In fact, in many ways, it's a victory. When I was a student at Columbia, I could've never predicted that I'd eventually want a career that was more family-oriented because kids weren't at the forefront of my plans back then.

I thought my professional career was an open and shut case—journalism all the way. But if it would've been that predictable, it wouldn't have had nearly the same excitement. I think this is just one example of how God knew my story long before I ever started writing it by dropping bread crumbs for me to follow along the way. Those crumbs led me to new career endeavors, and ultimately, greater happiness. Despite God's direction, though, it was my responsibility to determine what it meant to create a meaningful life. That meant I had to decide what's important to me. I had to decide who and what I was living for. What worked for me might not have worked for someone else. And that's okay. I learned that whatever I did, I needed to do it purposefully and passionately. And I needed to love it because life is too short for me to be sad, unfulfilled, or bored.

And that's one thing I've never been. My life, at least when you were young, seemed to be ever-changing, so I never had time to get bored. Just like I struggled with the decision to leave the news business, I found myself going through the fear of uncertainty again, just a few years later, after I finally had the family I'd been yearning for. When I decided I was finished having children, I became antsy and anxious because I realized I was nearing the end of a life chapter and had no clue what was written in the rest of the book.

When I was a kid, I would envision future life scenarios and act them out in role play. I remember "playing school" and pretending I was in college. I then pretended to have a job. I had an imaginary wedding. And I pushed around two little baby dolls in a stroller. But that's all I imagined. There was nothing after that, at least nothing I could come up with. Those events seemed like the most exciting to me. So, once I had all I ever imagined wanting, I was stumped about what came next.

I didn't feel the uneasiness after you were born because I knew I wanted to try to have another baby. But after Sissy's birth, the anxiety set in. Actually, the anticipation of the anxiety crept in just a few days before her arrival.

*It's Thursday. My baby girl will be here on Monday, if not before. Billy has already nicknamed her Sissy Bobo. I can't believe I'll have a daughter this time next week. Actually, I'll have a daughter in four days. That's insane and scary and exciting and overwhelming and happy and every emotion I could possibly feel. Sometimes when I haven't been thinking about this impending change for a minute, and then I think of it again, it doesn't seem real. It feels like it'll happen to someone else.*

*All of the flowers around town bloomed early this year. Usually they bloom in late March, but this year they bloomed weeks earlier for my sweet Sissy. It's like they're getting ready for her arrival, too. It's like the world already knows how special she is. Spring is so beautiful anyway, and it always makes me excited, and now it's even more beautiful and exciting knowing that from now on, it will represent her birth. All the azaleas are as perfect as they could possibly be…just like my sweet Sissy.*

*This pregnancy went by much faster than Billy's. I felt like I was pregnant for years with him. I feel like I just blinked with Sis. And it makes me sad, because this will probably be my last pregnancy, and I will never get this time in my life back. I'm already mourning the end of an era. I waited my whole life to have babies, and now that stage is over, and I'm sad.*

*I know I am meant to be more than just a baby-making machine. I have other purposes. Not that bringing a new life into this world isn't miraculous and arguably the best experience I'll ever have, but I know it's not the only exciting experience I'm meant to have. So while I'm sad it's over, I'm also anxious because I don't know what will come next. Will I finally write a book? Will I drown in a sea of dirty diapers? What will happen to me? I can't stand not knowing, and I feel a lot of pressure to figure it out.*

I think my fear stemmed from the fact that the first half of my life was very mapped out. I knew I wanted to graduate high school, attend college or find a trade, join the workforce, find a life partner, and create a family, and that's because most everyone I knew who was older than me did those exact same things. But I've found, after examining my own life, and looking at my older peers, it's sort of a crapshoot after the childbearing stage. I'd see moms who were focused solely on raising their children; moms who were climbing the professional ladder; moms who were struggling to figure out their next move. And that was my dilemma. When your daddy and I started dating and discussing the future, I told him that I hoped to one day have a son and a daughter. So once you and Sissy were born, Graff wanted to confirm that we were finished having kids, based on our previous conversation. One part of me was in agreement but the other part of me was undecided. Deep down, I knew that to end this chapter of my life, the last predictable chapter, meant I needed to figure out what else I wanted in my life, and in the meantime, embrace the unknown.

There was a brief period of time after Sissy was born that I wondered if I was truly finished having children. I was so confused. I had one friend who had two children, but knew she ultimately wanted four. So I secretly, and selfishly, dreaded the announcement of her next pregnancy because I worried it would make me sad if I'd decided I wouldn't be experiencing another one of my own. Anticipating her next child made me question my decision.

But I also had another friend who, after two children, immediately and confidently decided two was enough. On the days I'd fantasize about having another kid (because I'd attended a play date with the mom who wanted four), I'd then think about the mom who's happy with two and feel envious when I envisioned her enjoying carefree days with no diapers or 3 a.m. feedings while I was toting around a third baby and leaking breast milk. I imagined her riding happily atop a magical unicorn named Freedom, and I desperately wanted to hop on.

*Hi-ho, Freedom! Away!*

I'd ping-pong back and forth between the two moms until I ultimately decided I needed to do what was right for my own family and be as confident in my choice as they were with theirs.

The summer after Sissy was born represented the moment I realized my family was complete, and the moment I decided to see what the next chapter had in store. As I worked on this book, a project I hoped to one day give to my children, I sat on the front porch swing listening to the cicadas cheering me on. While writing about my hopes for the future, I discovered that I, a control-freak, was actually looking forward to a future less mapped out. I realized that I needed more spontaneity in my life, as accepting spontaneity gracefully was not one of my strengths. Because my previous chapters were so predictable, I had been accustomed to, and too dependent on, familiarity. And as a result, fear of the unknown and the thought of not having a plan, terrified me. I decided I would enjoy life more if I just "let go and let God." I wanted my next chapter to be filled with more self-discovery. I wanted you and Sissy to remember me as a mom who was actively engaged in your lives, but also as a mom who showed you it was important to have my own creative outlets, hobbies, and goals. You were my main focus, but it wasn't healthy for you to be my only focus.

My prayer for you is that you find happiness in whatever chapter you're in and embrace the gift of being able to create your own story. In my story, I'm thankful for the lessons I re-learned through my kids. Our favorite bedtime stories were always the ones with endings we never saw coming, where the main character learned very valuable life lessons—whether that was to never hold an angry alligator on live TV or that it's okay to change your dreams.

# Five

It was a cold December morning in the Lowcountry as Billy Rubin headed out to see Santa Clause (well, cold by South Carolina standards. It was actually sixty-two degrees, but to South Carolinians, that's cold, so Momma put on her parka).

Momma dressed Billy in a three-piece gray tweed suit with a red and black plaid shirt under the vest because she said it's important to wear your "Sunday best" when meeting the Big Guy.

In the car on the way there, Billy Rubin thought about Santa Clause (who he mistakenly called "Santa Closet"). He wasn't sure why Momma and Daddy continued to make him see Ol' Saint Nick every year. Truly, the man in the stained and stinky red velvet suit with the massive amounts of fake, yellowed facial hair and goofy hat was terrifying.

Once at the mall, they waited in line. When only one kid stood between Billy and Santa, Momma whipped out her camera and prepared to capture the magical moment on video.

Then, Billy told her he didn't want to sit on Santa's lap. Momma panicked. She asked what would make him feel comfortable enough to go up on the stage. Billy Rubin told her he'd only approach Santa if he could touch Santa's shiny boots and stand beside him. No lap-sitting.

Agreed.

Billy walked up to Santa and began petting his boot. Santa looked bewildered (and a little creeped out). Momma and Daddy made sure the video camera was recording and listened closely, waiting for Santa to ask Billy what he wanted for Christmas. They were eager to know. Momma thought he'd request a Power Wheels Jeep. Daddy staked his bet on a red bicycle.

"And what would you like for Christmas, little boy?" Santa asked in his loud, boisterous voice. He then quietly added, "Hey, kid, get your face off my boot."

"I want cheese," Billy Rubin said.

"Cheese?" Santa asked, confused.

"Mmmhmm," Billy Rubin replied. "Cheese."

Daddy laughed. Momma stood frozen in terror. How could he be the kid who wants cheese? Only cheese? She could've saved a lot of money by not buying the Power Wheels and instead opting for a package of Kraft Singles.

Billy, though, didn't care that it wasn't the typical response to Santa's question. He was being honest and genuine, and he truly would've been happier to receive cheese than anything else that Christmas. He was wowed by the little things (and the edible things, obviously), and he lived life just that simply: grateful for what he had while keeping his requests for what he wanted very minimal.

After the Santa Clause experience, Momma bought a cheese tray that contained a poem, perfectly articulating Billy's life motto written to mimic the lyrics of Eurythemics' "Sweet Dreams (Are Made of These)":

"Sweet dreams are made of cheese,
Who am I to diss a brie?
I cheddar the world, and the feta cheese,
Everybody's looking for Stilton."

WHEN YOU WERE GROWING UP, IF THE WEATHER WAS nice (above sixty-two degrees), you, Sissy, and I would go play on the swing set in our backyard after we ate our lunch. It was such a common occurrence back then that I took it for granted.

One day, though, after a particularly stressful morning, I was sitting in my usual spot—opposite you on the teeter-tot-ter—when you looked at me with your big, navy-blue eyes and said, "Momma, this is fun!" And that proclamation hit me hard—this *was* fun. And I had been missing it because I wasn't embracing the moment. I was usually guilty of thinking too far ahead: got to get the kids down for a nap so I can prep dinner kind-of-thing. That moment was entertaining, and my worries and fears and stresses in life were robbing me of this snapshot in time with my children. I learned that life moves fast, and I shouldn't speed it up by not being present.

It was such a profound moment for me that I told you we should thank God for it. We thanked Him not only for the fun we were having, but also for my ability to be home during lunch time with you and Sissy. It was something I'd hoped for, but didn't know if it would happen.

Though I'm grateful for my time in the news business, the hours were grueling, and I yearned for more freedom and flexibility professionally. After working in TV for those six years, I was ready to try something new. My entire last year in news, I cried every day on the way to the station because I was so miserable with my job. I realized being a journalist matched my skill set, but not my personality type. Meaning, I was good at my job, but the requirements made me sad. I always felt like I was putting someone's worst day on TV for everyone to see. "Your son was murdered.... Can I interview you?" "Your daughter was kidnapped....Can I interview you?" "Your house just burned to the ground....Can I interview you?" I, in no way, want to discredit all the good things the media does for the public. I believe, oftentimes, the public benefits from the news business as it keeps us informed and highlights the beauty in the world, but I was unhappy with my role because I felt it focused mainly on the negative aspects of the job, and I needed a change.

Realizing that my career wasn't the right fit was the seed that led to me creating my own business. Opening a college planning firm with a mission of finding students compatible college majors was my way of filling a need I saw in our community (and within myself), and I hoped it would lead my clients to contentment within their future careers.

I remember my first day at the "office"—the dining room table. I had no clue where to start. I sat there for hours, staring at my computer, writing a few notes, and panicking. Completely at a loss, I opened my Bible—just opened it, not really searching for any particular verse. And the first one I laid eyes on was Matthew 17:20-23, which reads, "I tell you the truth, if you have faith the size of a mustard seed, you can say to that mountain, 'Move from here to there,' and it will move. Nothing will be impossible for you."

Using a red ink pen, I wrote that verse on an index card and put it in a picture frame. I sat the frame in front of me on the table.

The next day, staring at the red ink, I came up with a name for the business: Landmark 12 Consulting. I chose "Landmark" because it was a landmark decision in my life to start the business, and I'd be helping students make their first landmark decisions. And I chose "12" because I wanted to try to live like Jesus' twelve disciples, who were called to do things that intimidated them, yet they still obeyed. I felt like God wanted me to help others and this was the avenue to do it. I certainly didn't feel worthy of, or prepared for, such a task, but as my pastor at the time used to say, "God doesn't always call the qualified; He qualifies the called."

I chose the number "12" for other reasons, too. Twelve has a lot of significance in the Bible. In Matthew 5:21, it's written that Jesus heals a woman who had been sick for twelve years and raises a twelve-year-old girl from the dead. I figured that since he performed these astounding miracles, he could certainly help a clueless former-journalist figure out how to start a business.

Leaving the news industry and deciding to not have any more children were among the hardest decisions of my life, but starting a business was one of the easiest. I was passionate about my mission and eager to get started. However, even though the decision was uncomplicated, the execution and the aftermath were not. And that challenging time was sandwiched right in between the two other challenging life events—deciding to leave news and the births of my babies.

Not even a month after your daddy and I decided I should quit my job as a journalist to concentrate on writing my business plan, I found out I was pregnant with you. I found myself creating a business…and a family…at the same time.

After the initial excitement of starting a business (and discovering I was going to be a momma) subsided, it was time to get down to work. Both life events required planning, and going through both at once was hard. I found that creating my business could be broken into three parts: research and development; training and marketing; launching and maintaining. And, ironically, I found the three stages of the business coincided with my pregnancy trimesters: I founded my business and learned of my pregnancy in the same month; I named you and Landmark 12 in the same week; Landmark 12 was officially launched and "born" in July, and you arrived just a few weeks later in August.

As you grew, so did my company.

While I know that the two life events can't truly be compared (for me, there's no greater gift and privilege than to become a mother), I do think of my company as a "baby" of sorts, and it's always held a special place in my heart. Just like with you, I watched Landmark 12 learn to crawl in its infancy, then eventually it gained the strength to walk, and now, it can run.

Never have I learned so much—about myself, about business, about life. The most important lesson the business taught me is to never assume your dreams can't be your reality. If you work hard, push through the difficult times, and keep running with your ambitions, you'll eventually arrive at your destination. And here's the second most important lesson: Sometimes that destination is different than what you thought it would be when you started the journey due to all the twists, turns, and surprises…and that's okay. You can't possibly predict the exact outcome when you take that leap of faith. How boring would that be?

For me, the best things in my life took nine months to create. But the time leading up to the company "running" was so hard. Your daddy worked two jobs to supplement our income until the business picked up. He'd leave his job in corporate finance every day to then go park vehicles at a rental car company. We will always affectionately refer to Avis as "Save-Us." There were many evenings, home alone with you, a new baby, that I'd cry myself to sleep before Graff got home. I felt guilty for putting my time into a business that may never thrive and get him out of his current situation. He never once complained, though. He never once said the job was beneath him. He never once told me that I had to stop trying and go back to a job I hated.

On the nights I didn't cry myself to sleep, I'd write in my journal. One night, I wrote a letter to your dad, but never gave it to him.

*I feel like we haven't gotten to talk much lately. Not on a deeper level, anyway. I feel like our conversations for the past month have mainly been about poopy diapers and spit-up and whatever cute/gross thing Billy is doing at the time. Our world is so completely different, and I don't want to forget to talk about it.*

*Mainly, I'm just afraid of losing "us." You are trying so hard. And please know that I recognize that. Sometimes I worry that in my struggle to survive these past few weeks, I've forgotten to tell you you're the reason I have survived and how truly grateful I am. Don't think I don't recognize the little things you do (in addition to the big things like getting up with Billy throughout the night when I was sick). One little thing that always makes me feel good is the notes you write me. I know that's your way of trying to build me up during this time I've been down and your way of not losing "us." It helps, but I still worry. We always say, "Let's talk about _____ when you get home," but I don't feel like we ever do. When you get home, we're both exhausted and we do very little real talking. That is no one's fault, but it's something I hope we both can work on.*

*You just left to go to Avis, and I'm feeling the same empty, sad feeling I always feel when you leave. Don't get me wrong, I think alone time is great. But the problem is that I feel like I'm always alone. I feel guilty for saying that because I have this beautiful baby boy sitting here with me, but I still feel alone. And I feel guilty because it's raining. I hate that you go to work in the rain. I hate that I can't make the situation better for us. I wish more than anything I could figure out how to get more clients quickly so that you could leave Avis. I know you hate working two jobs. I know you're the one who should be complaining, not me. But you never do. That just speaks to your dedication to our family and your work ethic. But it also makes me feel like I shouldn't complain or that I'm a bad, weak person if I do.*

*Please know how eternally grateful I am for everything you've done, and are currently doing, for our family. Not many men would work seven days a week, two jobs, so that their wives could start their own business. You saved me. I just wish I could now save you. I can't imagine what it's like for you to work so much. For me, I get sad because without a day off with you, the weeks just drag on and on and on. It seems like one long, miserable week. And I'm not even the one working. I lose track of the days, and I feel like I have nothing to look forward to. I miss you.*

*I feel guilty for complaining about anything at all because I know that we are blessed. Times are tough for us, and we struggle, but we've been given many gifts, and I don't want to sound like I don't recognize that. A healthy baby boy is a gift from God. That's why I feel bad when I complain about his crying. I feel like I'm letting God down, as well as you and Billy and myself. I feel like maybe I'm not a good mom. I know you say I can't make that judgment in the first month of parenthood, but it's hard not to. I've waited my whole life to be a mother, and to be honest, I'm miserable.*

*Nothing has really been a surprise for me. I knew a baby would require twenty-four-seven care. I knew babies cried a lot. I knew it would be tough to start a business while also starting a family. I knew all of that. But it's been much harder for me to handle than I thought it would be. I guess I didn't truly know what I was getting myself into. And now, of course, I have no choice but to deal with it all. But I'm not doing a very good job of dealing with it, and that bothers me.*

*I hope Billy and I can settle into a routine. I hope that I can somehow become more patient. I hope that I can get more clients. I hope that you can leave Avis before the end of the year. I hope that life isn't always like this for us. We always seem to be struggling. I hope that we don't always have to watch every dollar we spend. I hope that one day I can buy something without first checking our bank account and then feeling guilty about the purchase afterward. I hope that we can get cable again one day. I hope I don't have post-partum depression. I hope I can function normally again soon. I hope that Billy doesn't sense my frustration with him. I hope that he loves me. I hope that I eventually feel like myself…even though I think I've forgotten what that felt like because it's been so long. I hope that Billy and the business are the last big changes we have for a while. I miss normalcy. I hope you and I can be close again. I feel like I'm losing you between caring for Billy and you working so much. I hope I can get through just one day without crying. I hope it stops raining because you don't deserve to have to work in the rain. I hope some of my hopes come true.*

*I know I keep saying this, but I can't stop thinking that I've spent the past month struggling to survive. I felt like I was struggling to physically survive the hottest cicada summer I've ever experienced, while visiting Mamaw's grave in my third trimester; then, I was mentally struggling in the hospital after Billy was born when I realized my world had just changed forever; and now, I'm struggling to keep it together emotionally. Sometimes I just sit here and close my eyes, like I did when I was in labor, and try to talk myself off the cliff, tell myself that everything is okay, and that I'll get through this. In those moments, I don't feel like I'm living. I'm merely surviving. And I hate that.*

*Sometimes I get my phone and go out on the porch and start to call someone, just so I don't feel so alone. But then I realize I don't really have anyone to call. And then I feel worse. Sometimes, without even realizing what I'm doing, I think about calling Mamaw, which then makes me sad once I catch myself thinking it.*

*It's only 7:17. You've only been at work for an hour and seventeen minutes, but it seriously feels like ten hours to me. I can't wait for you to get home.*

I have always been a worrier. It's one of my biggest faults. I waste an insane amount of time worrying about everything, and it's in those moments that I have to remember to give it to God. Graff's time with Avis was another instance in my life where I put all my faith in God. I had no other reason to believe my business would be successful other than because I felt called to do it. Just like with my New York experience, and after losing Mamaw, and finding such a supportive life partner in Graff, I had to trust God's plan and not let my fear of the unknown stop me from plowing forward.

Coming out the other side of that dark, uncertain time makes the memory of the moment with you on the teeter-totter even more magical—life could've very easily gone the other way. The business could've never gotten off the ground. Hardships, expected or unexpected, are inevitable. The gift lies within the lessons learned.

After you went off to preschool, the business had grown substantially, and I decided to leave the dining room table and open an office. One week after moving into commercial space, I found out I was pregnant with Sissy, and the business continued to grow right along with you two. I remember watching sweet Sissy, with her shiny, strawberry-blonde hair and sky-blue eyes, blow bubbles in the yard while you yelled, "Higher, Momma, higher!" on the teeter-totter, and feeling contentment and appreciation. We don't always notice a bright spot after a dark time. Things don't always work out the way we want them to. That's life. So when things do fall into place, it makes it even sweeter. The innocence I remember seeing in your eyes, and the genuineness in your laughter, was a constant reminder of how wonderful life can be. It was a reminder to bow my head, right then, and thank God for everything—those wonderful moments, the strife I overcame, the past pain that made me grateful for my current happiness, and the security of knowing God would be with me during my next challenge.

My prayer for you is that you take time to feel appreciative for where you are in life. Right now, this very moment. Things could be, and probably have been, worse. Stop right now, and smell the roses (or in your case, smell the cheese).

# Six

It was a bright, sunny day in the Lowcountry, but Billy Rubin didn't feel so bright and sunny. In fact, he had been sick with a tummy ache for several days.

Momma and Daddy took him to the doctor even though Billy hated going to the doctor. After screaming uncontrollably for several minutes (the nurse was only trying to check his temperature), the doctor told them that Billy had a stomach virus. He said the virus just had to run its course, but that the main concern was the diaper rash Billy had developed due to excessive diarrhea. He suggested allowing Billy, who was not potty-trained, to spend time without a diaper on to "let his buttocks air out."

Nearly a decade of medical school and this was what he came up with.

Momma and Daddy took the doctor's advice, though, because, as first-time parents, they were idiots. They promptly returned home, freed Billy's buttocks, and started making dinner: a bland, tasteless concoction of chicken and rice they hoped would make Billy's tummy feel better. After all, it was Billy's world, and they were just living in it. Even though Billy still wasn't feeling well, he was loving life running around the house without diaper on. Just as daddy turned off the stove, he turned around to see Billy slyly exiting the kitchen, leaving a trail of crap on the floor. Daddy followed the trail back to its place of origin: the kitchen pantry. In the pantry, there was the biggest pile of poop he'd ever seen.

Momma walked downstairs and was nearly knocked over by the odor of the bland, tasteless crap Daddy made for dinner combined with the smell of actual crap that was now all over the floor. She immediately noticed the Billy Rubin-sized footprints, coated in poop, exiting the kitchen and venturing toward her new rug in the living room. As she peeked her head around the corner, horror of horrors, she spotted another pile on her brand-new rug while Black-Eyed Hollie was chasing Billy Rubin's freshly-soiled butt.

Billy Rubin and Momma locked eyes. He looked helpless. She looked horrified. It was then that Billy learned a very valuable, very tough life lesson: Shit happens. Yes, sweet, Billy—In this crazy life, shit happens, and as much as it stinks, you must deal with it.

Billy wasted no time, though, turning crappy into happy. He looked at his situation as an opportunity to play a game of chase with Black-Eyed Hollie and jump on Daddy's back and ride him like a horse, as Daddy was on his hands and knees scooping poop out of the pantry. This was a glorious day, in fact, and there was no need to let life's crap get him down.

BEFORE YOU WERE BORN, WHEN LIFE TOOK A DUMP ON me, my first reaction was usually not to embrace it, let alone turn it into a positive situation like you did that day. As an adult, I knew part of that job description was to be able to handle what life threw at me, because everyone will undoubtedly encounter their fair share of difficulties, but for some reason, I always assumed I had more crap to deal with than anyone else. Woe is me. I'd think, what did I do to deserve this? And then I'd have a pity party. I still occasionally have pity parties (hey, I'm human), but I notice they don't last as long as they once did. They're more like pity get-togethers instead of full-blown soirees. Now, every time I face a challenge, I smile thinking about you, and appreciate your ability to overcome a less-than-ideal situation. You recovered from embarrassment and fear with grace and humor. If only I could always be that brave.

Another problem that stems from crappy situations: entitlement. We've all been in a difficult situation, and after we overcome it, we think, well now that I've had to deal with that, I shouldn't have to deal with anything else. Like we've met our quota of crap.

Unfortunately, life doesn't work that way. I've found that in my life, the crap comes in waves. It's almost certain that if something extra-challenging happens, it will be followed by equally challenging events as if to test my strength or endurance, or most importantly, my faith.

I'd like to think you (and your sister) have shown me what truly matters in life. Yes, it's important to handle the tough times with dignity and humility, with your head held high, but it's also important to be able to put life into perspective. In the grand scheme of things, is this instance really that big of a deal? If it is, deal with it. If it's not, step in the shit and move on. Being weighed down by insignificant baggage is no way to live. For me, it's only generated a lot of negative emotions (stress, dislike, jealousy, anger, sadness) and robbed me of positive emotions that make me my best self.

Let me tell you about a time when I wasn't my best self: those early years of motherhood.

It was an ugly sight and was anything but graceful and natural and beautiful (as I assumed it would be).

I remember my friend, who didn't have children, coming to see you when you were a week old. After she gushed over you for a few minutes, I asked my friend how she was doing, in an effort to hear about normal life outside of motherhood for a moment. Her response: "Ugh, actually, I'm not feeling so great today. I think I got too much sleep last night."

My sleep-deprived brain found this insanely funny. I knew what she meant, but it seemed so far removed from my life; I was positive I'd never experience a decent amount, let alone an excessive amount, of sleep again.

I thought, *Sleep? What's sleep?! I'm over here surviving on Mountain Dew and Jesus.*

After she left, I couldn't get to my journal fast enough. I was desperate to write down my thoughts and try to make sense of my new life.

*I feel like I'm swimming in an unfamiliar world. It's so bizarre. I can't describe it. It's unlike anything I've ever experienced, and I know I'm drowning. I keep thinking I'm going to wake up and realize it was all a dream.*

*I'm starting to, slowly, learn how to take care of Billy. I'm not sure I truly understand how to be a mother yet. I kind of just feel like a babysitter. I've learned what makes him cry and how to (somewhat) prevent that; how to change a diaper; how to feed and burp him. But I'm struggling with how I teach him life lessons. When does that begin? I can't even remember to stop cussing, let alone teach him something meaningful.*

*I talk to him. I wonder if that makes a difference? I tell him what the agenda looks like each day; what color the sky is; what he's wearing; what the dog is doing in the yard. What stimulates this little creature? Tummy-time? A book? Micky Mouse Clubhouse? Hell if I know.*

*I'm trying to figure out how to incorporate my work schedule into his play/eat/crap schedule. I think I've made some improvements from last week, but am still not there yet. I remember being pregnant and writing over and over again how I couldn't imagine working and raising a newborn. I'm slowly learning how. I just wish the process was faster.*

*Sometimes I forget that I'm not pregnant. That entire experience had a profound impact on my life. For some reason, it's hard for me to get over it. My brain is struggling. When I feel a cramp in my belly, for a second, I think it's the baby kicking.*

*Speaking of that, it is so bizarre to watch him kick right now and know he once did that inside of me. It's crazy to think that he was inside me at all. That's so creepy and miraculous…all at the same time.*

*Graff and I took Billy to a restaurant with us for the first time on Saturday. It was a reminder of just how different our life has become. We had to leave quickly to avoid a Billy Rubin meltdown and feed him in the parking lot. We had to change Billy's poopy diaper in the backseat of the Pontiac. Instead of enjoying dinner and being able to drive away immediately after we were finished, we had to rush out of the restaurant and tend to the baby for thirty minutes. Everything in our life takes so much longer and is so much more dramatic. Sometimes I feel like I'm mourning the loss of our old life. And then I feel guilty. When I think about how much I miss the simplicity of life and being able to just focus on Graff and myself, it makes me think that I'm a bad mother. Or that I'm not maternal. Like right now, I want to finish writing in my journal but Billy smells like crap, so I know I need to change his diaper. But he's sleeping, and it's a rare moment of silence, so I'm wondering if it makes me a bad mom to just let him lay in shit for a minute?*

The dilemmas a new parent faces are like none other. Still to this day, when I think back on those first few days, weeks, and months of motherhood, it feels like I'm struggling to remember a dream. My sleep deprivation at the time plays a part in that, I'm sure. But it also feels like my brain blocked it out, or lessened the intensity of those moments, on purpose, almost like a coping mechanism for me. I'm most certain that's how parents decide to conceive again. This world would have no second children if parents vividly remembered the exhausting, terrifying moments they experienced with their first.

Speaking of coping mechanisms, I am also convinced there's a reason children do not remember their first few years of life. Parents screw up so royally during those first years, it's best kids don't have a recollection. It might scar them for life. It's like God gave us a buffer zone. We got a pass. We got a period of time to get our shit together and figure out how to appropriately raise these tiny humans.

What I do remember is spending a lot of time writing. Looking back, I probably felt ashamed of my inability to function and didn't want to confide those feelings in family and friends. New mothers shouldn't feel guilty; in fact, I make it a point to tell new mothers about struggles I went through, not to scare them but to let them know that life will feel different and disjointed, but it will ultimately become a new normal, and happiness will live there.

*The week started off really rough but gradually got better. I nearly had a breakdown on Monday. Billy wouldn't stop crying while I was trying to work. He was fussy all day. I didn't get to eat lunch. So then I got a migraine. I had to have Graff come home from work early just so I could take a shower in peace. I thought I was losing my mind. It occurred to me while in the shower that I didn't take a shower the previous day. So, now I'm crazy…and I have poor hygiene. What has my life become?*

*At some point during the week, I learned I can't make Billy work within my schedule. I have to work within his. Unfortunately, that means I now use the term "schedule" very loosely. And I have to be very strategic. If I need to bathe him or change him, but he's sleeping, I just let him sleep. And instead, I'll do all the other things I had to do that don't pertain to him. If I need to work but he's being fussy, I just tend to him and work when he falls asleep. It can be frustrating to have one person dictate my entire day, but I am starting to get used to it. I'm beginning to feel like I'm doing more than just surviving. I'm starting to en- joy motherhood. I think it comes from a combination of feeling better and getting better at being a mother. On Monday, I had no patience and could barely look at him when he was crying be- cause I was so mad. Today, I hold him when he cries and want to provide comfort. I'm not saying I'll never get frustrated again, but I'm definitely having more good days currently.*

*Somehow, Graff and I are still trucking along, and a month has gone by since Billy was born. I'm not sure how we sur- vived it at times, but we did. Everyone says the first few months are the hardest, and we already have one under our belts. The sleepless nights might kill us, though, so hopeful- ly they'll be over soon. I'm very conflicted with my feelings. Part of me wants Billy to be older so he can sleep better. But another part of me knows he'll only be my tiny baby for a short period of time, and I need to cherish it.*

*I get sad when I think of Billy growing up. I bet I'll battle that my entire life. I do look forward to him being able to communicate with me. And I look forward to him running and playing and going on family vacations. But for the most part, I wish I could freeze time.*

*I do think I'm taking advantage of our time together as much as possible. I hold him a lot. I stare at him. This morning, I was rocking him in the chair in his room, and my brain kept telling my body to go dust the furniture downstairs, but my heart wouldn't let me put my baby down. I wanted to savor the moment.*

I'm not sure if it's because I had you, my first child, a little later in life than some of my friends, or if it's just because I'm stubborn (or a combination of both), but I had a very hard time accepting that another human could dictate my entire day (and my life for the foreseeable future). I lived totally by myself for eight years and then lived with just your daddy for two, so for a decade, I was accustomed to only caring for myself or one other (mostly) self-sufficient adult.

Another issue I struggled with was the hijacking of my brain. Between much less sleep, and much more craziness, I realized that my mind was legitimately not as sharp as it was before I had kids. No joke. When you were three, I walked into your preschool classroom and overheard one of the other mothers telling the teacher that her son's "Show and Tell" item was in his bookbag. Show and Tell? I didn't know there was

Show and Tell that day. So I asked your teacher for confirmation, and she told me that every Friday was Show and Tell with the letter the students were learning about that week; you were supposed to bring in an item that started with the letter *F*. You do the math. Somehow, I'd obliviously missed five weeks of Show and Tell. I felt horrible—you'd had nothing to show for letters *A* through *E*. I frantically started searching in my purse for something that started with the letter *F* to give to you. I found fake eyelashes (don't ask), fiber laxatives (again, don't ask), and a Fruit Loop (because that's what I am). Then, your teacher said, "Don't worry, we figured he wouldn't have anything again this week, so we told him to just show his fingers."

Show his fingers? Show his fingers. Wow. I wanted to show one of my fingers.

When it came to parenting, I was either nailing it or failing it. There was no in between. And on that day, I was definitely failing. Hey, there's an *F* word for you.

And I can also think of one more…

Faith! (What did you think I was going to say? Shame on you!) I just needed to keep the faith.

I may have realized that my processing and thinking abilities were not what they used to be, but I also recognized my multi-tasking skills were through the roof—way better than they were before I had kids. I could be parked in the pick-up line at school, breastfeeding a baby, making a grocery list, eating a banana, and dancing to the Van Morrison song on the radio. Take that, pre-baby self.

Speaking of the pick-up line, I would frequently park behind a Pontiac Transport minivan filled with toddler triplets and a mom who routinely still had one rogue curler tangled in her hair, looking like she could take a nap for five days, and the bumper sticker on the back of the van read: "I used to be cool."

That's definitely how I felt. Parenting was a constant give-and-take for me—readjusting who I was and transforming into the new model I needed to become in a different phase of life. As adults, our super powers are constantly changing. When I was in college, my super power was guessing correctly on multiple-choice exams that I didn't study for. In my days as a poor, young journalist, my super power was learning how to survive on the twelve dollars I had left in my checking account in the week and a half until pay day. As a young parent, I would pride myself on being that mom parked in the school pick-up line nonchalantly dominating the domestics. That's the part of life that no one tells you about. That's the part you can never truly prepare for. That's the part that gives you the bumps, bruises, and scars that you'll talk about from your rocking chair in the retirement home. It's the part you never really wanted but will miss the most.

My prayer for you is that in those moments when you're reminded just how messy life can be, you embrace it. Pray. Laugh if you can. Cry if you must. And buckle up. Because sometimes, throughout this journey, all you're surviving on is Mountain Dew and Jesus.

# Seven

BILLY RUBIN HAD A ROTTEN DAY. HE WOKE UP IN THE morning not feeling quite like himself. Not only was he feeling sleepy and not wanting to get out of bed, his pajama pants literally felt different...he had peed the bed. Not a fun way to start the morning. To make matters worse, he had peed all over his best buddy, Hobbes, who was his favorite stuffed giraffe and his sleeping companion.

Breakfast didn't improve his spirits. Momma gave him milk. Billy didn't want milk, but instead of politely declining his usual morning drink, he threw his milk cup across the kitchen. Momma made him sit in his timeout chair where he cried some more. Momma asked why he was crying, and he said he was upset because he actually did want to drink some milk. Life is confusing.

After breakfast, Momma had some bad news: She had put Hobbes in the washer because he smelled like pee, and when she pulled him out, she noticed his ear had fallen off. Billy was mad.

As if the morning hadn't been hard enough, there was more bad news: Potty training was continuing. Billy hated learning to use the potty. Momma took away his diaper and made him wear "big boy undies" with Ninja Turtles on them. Billy wanted his diaper back. When Momma made him sit on the potty, he threw the toilet paper, broke the flusher, and refused to pee or poop. He had to go back to his timeout chair.

Around lunch time, Billy pooped in his Ninja Turtle underwear. It was yucky for everyone involved.

When Momma took Billy grocery shopping, Billy declared, "I don't want to behave in the store. I want to be naughty." And he was being serious. Billy knocked aspirin and vitamin bottles off the shelves (as Momma shopped for extra-strength headache medicine).

Back in the center aisle, walking through the main part of the store, Billy suddenly yelled, "Feed me! I'm hungry because you haven't feeded me since last week! I'm a starving boy!"

Shoppers shot Momma horrified, disgusted stares.

Desperate for some peace, Momma frantically searched her diaper bag for a snack and pulled out crackers. The starving boy only ate one.

Finally, in the check-out line, the cashier, who was handing out free cookies, asked if Billy had been a good boy that day, and if he deserved a treat. He decided to fess up to his numerous wrongdoings, and the cashier looked troubled. She decided to give his cookie to Momma, who then decided to save it for after dinner. Billy made a mental note to lie to the cashier next time.

Even though Billy had been sleepy all day, he refused to take a nap. That made him even crankier.

After play time, he refused to pick up his toys because he was too tired. Momma made him do it anyway. He threw a fit (and his train set). He had to go back to the timeout chair.

At dinner, he made sure to scarf down all of his chicken and vegetables because he wanted to eat that cookie the cashier had given to Momma. She put it on his placemat in front of him, but in a split second, Hollie jumped up on the chair next to Billy and snatched his prized treat.

After that, Billy Rubin was ready for bed. He actually climbed in by himself without Momma or Daddy telling him to. Momma handed Hobbes to him—with a freshly re-attached ear. That turned the entire day around for Billy. It might've been a rotten day, but at the end of it, everyone had survived and everything was intact. Somehow, he instinctively knew that while it might've been a bad day, life goes on, and tomorrow will be better. He also learned a very important lesson: Sometimes in life, you just need to throw your fit and take your time-out. Then keep on moving forward.

MY ENTIRE LIFE TOOK A TIME-OUT FOR EXACTLY FIVE months after you were born. I explained in the last chapter that I didn't adjust easily to motherhood. At first, I assumed I was going through the adjustment period, and its growing pains, that all new parents experience. But after the first month, when I found it nearly impossible to get out of bed and felt resentment toward you for forcing me out, I knew I had more than just post-baby blues—I was suffering from post-partum depression.

Even though I realized after that first month that something wasn't quite right, it took a while for me to acknowledge that I needed help. I wanted to think that I could fix the situation on my own. I'd always heard the feelings of post-partum sufferers usually revolved around wanting to harm oneself or the baby. And I didn't feel that way. So I assumed climbing out of the hole I was in would be easy. But it wasn't.

No one in my life talked much about post-partum depression. If other moms I knew went through it, they never clued me in. Once I did start talking to people about it, I got the impression that it was something I wasn't supposed to be sharing, like I should keep it a secret. There was a stigma surrounding it that made it seem like the moms who talked about it were weak or didn't love their children.

So my feelings only lived in my journal.

*The one thing that's really hard to get used to is having to cater to someone twenty-four-seven. Regardless of whether I feel like it or not, I have to be there for him. And I'll be honest, sometimes I don't want to be. Sometimes I want to stay in bed instead. Sometimes I want to be able to eat before I have to feed him. And I often wonder if that makes me a bad mom. Sometimes I get so damn tired of hearing him cry and scream. He's been way more fussy than usual lately, and I'm just not sure sometimes if I have the strength and the patience to deal with it.*

*I've had such a frustrating week. Billy had a horrible day on Wednesday. He shrieked like a dying cat for what seemed like hours. I cried. A lot. And then on top of everything else I was feeling, I felt guilty for not being more patient with him. He spit up on me eight times that day. I had vomit running down in between my boobs. I was covered in rancid stomach bile, yet he was screaming at me? I wanted to scream at him. I tried to soak in the tub to scrub off the first vomit incident. But as soon as I sat down, his vibrating chair stopped vibrating and he started screaming and I thought, deep breaths, deep breaths....*

*I asked Graff to come home early from work again. At the time, I thought it was the only way I'd be able to survive the day. But now I feel guilty because we needed that money. Sometimes I fantasize about getting in my car and driving away. The only thing that stops me is I'm always too tired to figure out where to go.*

*I think I have PPD. I had hoped and prayed that I wouldn't get it, but I need to acknowledge there's an issue. It's not that I don't love Billy. I just don't know if I love being a mother yet. It's not personal. My feelings aren't specific to him. He's a very good baby (despite Wednesday), but I just think it's been harder than I thought it would be to juggle it all. I haven't mastered it yet, and from what I'm hearing, I probably never will. I worry that I'm not patient and flexible enough to be a parent.*

I wish there hadn't been such a stigma around post-partum depression. Having gone through it, I realize it didn't make me a weak person or a bad mother. In fact, I think it made me a stronger, better mother than if I hadn't gone through that experience at all because I loved you enough to want help, and I forever kept myself, and my feelings, in check. For me, it took prayer, medication, and talk therapy to get back on track. And it didn't happen overnight. But I got through it, and when Sissy was born, I had a much better experience.

I think the biggest difference between Sissy's birth and yours is that with hers, I was better prepared for change. And the change didn't rock my world the way it did when you were born. Going from one kid to two is much easier, in my opinion, than going from none to one. I think the biggest contributor to my depression was my inability to roll with change. Even though I was expecting the change, I didn't accept it gracefully. I wanted a baby more than anything, yet when you came, I struggled with adjusting to my new life. The change that comes with first-time parenthood is epic.

That was my other problem. Mentally, I had a hard time accepting my needs would never be first again. I was selfish. Parenthood zaps the selfishness out of a person really quickly, and that can be a big adjustment. It was also selfish of me to feel resentment toward you when I saw your daddy putting all of his energy into you instead of showing me the attention he once did. Motherhood is a truly beautiful thing, but it definitely brought out my ugly side. It showed me insecurities and imperfections I'd never acknowledged, let alone addressed, before. I will always consider motherhood my greatest blessing—not just because of the amazing gifts of two children, but also because it taught me how to be a better person so I could then be a better mom.

When you were a baby, my goal, at least in those first five months, was to survive the day. With Sissy, my goal was to seize the day. There were moments when I was holding Sissy that I wished I could've turned back the clock and embraced more moments like that with you. I'm sorry. I do feel guilty I didn't feel that way with you at first, but I promise you, I spent the rest of your childhood trying to be the best mom I could be. And truly, during my post-partum depression, I was being the best mom I could be. I was struggling, but I acknowledged it and sought help. Don't ever be afraid to speak up if your burden is becoming too much to shoulder (whatever that burden may be). During my PPD, and truly, during every event in my life both good and bad, prayer was the shining light. Because let's face it—parenting is hard. Really hard. Sometimes I felt like prayer was all I had to hold on to when the madness of raising kids was swirling around me. Sometimes, and this is no joke, I'd hide from you and Sissy in the pantry just to eat some Oreos in peace and to thank God for the invention of that chocolatey perfection (and the much-needed time to decompress).

And I'd do it again in a heartbeat. If hiding in the pantry from kids is wrong, I don't want to be right.

Sometimes, those were the most calming forty-seven seconds of my day. I didn't care if those moments of peace were in a dark pantry...I wanted to break apart the cookie and lick the icing in solitude. There. I said it. And I don't feel guilty about it. In fact, I encourage you to find your happy place and retreat there when life approaches the cliff.

Overcoming PPD, and other hardships, taught me coping skills I would use during the next storm. Because, in life, there will always be another storm. Looking back on your childhood, some days, I was killing it—you and Sissy were immaculately dressed, walking into school on time, with a homecooked meal in your lunch boxes. Other days, I'd put the phone in the fridge and the butter in my purse. That's life, which wasn't always graceful, but was always grace-filled.

My prayer for you is that you take it easy on yourself—perfection isn't the goal. Count your blessings, and be appreciative of them. Focus on what's going right instead of what's wrong. Take a cue from your former self: If you poop in your Ninja Turtle underwear, slap on a new pair and start over. Here's the beauty in a bad day: The sun will come up again tomorrow, and you can always grab a fresh pair of undies.

# Eight

BILLY RUBIN, WITH HIS INNOCENT EYES AND WIDE smile, was a mischief magnet. Trouble found him wherever he went. It was hard for Momma to be mad at Billy because he was such a charmer. He'd flash that gap-toothed grin at her, and despite her frustration, she'd struggle to stifle a laugh.

Billy and Sissy Bobo were great at getting into mischief. Much to Momma's dismay, Billy had started calling his adorable younger sister "Yucky Dickens" because she was always making some kind of disgusting mess that Billy would later exacerbate.

Their favorite book was Dr. Seuss' *Cat in the Hat*. Billy and Sissy squealed every time the Cat balanced himself on a ball while holding an armful of household items—everything from a cake and an umbrella to a tray of milk and a fish bowl. This was the Cat's idea of fun even though it could potentially get the kids in trouble.

One day, Billy decided his idea of fun would be to raid the pantry, eating all the cookies and chips, and when Momma saw the mess, he'd blame it on Black-Eyed Hollie. He figured if the Cat in the Hat could be successfully sneaky, so could he. Billy didn't plan to offer his sister any treats because he figured

Yucky Dickens would be content just rolling around in the crumbs of his pantry raid.

When Momma wasn't looking, Billy pushed a stool into the pantry so he could reach his beloved treats and began throwing down the Lays and Oreos. Billy hopped off the stool, ripped open the packages, and shoved the food into his mouth while sitting comfortably in the pantry. He enticed Hollie to join using a half-chewed cookie. But much to Billy's chagrin, the joke wasn't just on Hollie. Sissy had nonchalantly crawled to the pantry door and slammed it closed, trapping both Hollie *and* Billy inside. Then she crawled far away from the chaos, pretending to not be involved when Momma discovered her pantry a wreck.

The pantry smelled of grease, chocolate, and regret. Hollie was angry because Billy had dropped a soup can on his head. Billy was crying because a frightened Hollie had bitten his butt in retaliation.

It was in that moment, Billy learned two valuable lessons: First, life (and Hollie) will bite you in the butt if given the chance. Second, much like the Cat and the Hat, this life is filled with characters just waiting to cause a little chaos. Sissy was Billy's chaos. As much as this first-born child hated to admit it, his younger sister could outwit him at every turn. He decided that the next time he wanted to be sneaky, he would let her be the mayhem-maven, the brainchild, and he would just be the mayhem-magnet. After all, in this life, if you decide to make a mess and get your hands dirty, there's no better person to do it with than Yucky Dickens.

Sissy would cause the light-hearted chaos in your life, and most people have someone, or something, that generates upheaval in their worlds, whether on a large or small scale; it can be in a fun way like with Sissy or in a more serious way like the memory of a traumatic event, which is the case for me.

Tomorrow is a new day. But sometimes in life, chaos can last for a season, not twenty-four hours, and it can teach us many lessons.

Do you remember the time your daddy and I took you to the fire museum? I was expecting to see replicas of vintage fire engines, but I didn't expect there to be full-blown fire simulators depicting a burning apartment building with smoke and animated people hanging from the windows screaming for help. You and I were terrified.

You were obviously scared because you hated loud sirens, but I was terrified because what I was looking at was all too real to me.

I've never told you this, but a few months after Mamaw died, during my senior year at Marshall, the apartment building I was living in caught on fire and looked eerily similar to the one we saw that day at the museum. The fire happened the night of my twenty-second birthday. Ordinarily, on a Friday night, I'd be in bed by nine o'clock because I got up extremely early for my 3 a.m. shift at the TV station. But I'd requested off for the night of my birthday, and I was at a comedy club with my friends when, during the middle of the show, the club manager suddenly hopped on the stage and announced there was an apartment fire spanning an entire city block just a few streets away.

I instinctively knew my life was about to change.

Because I was at a comedy club, for a split second, I questioned if this information was a sick joke.

I bolted out the door. My face was blasted with the thick, heavy smell of smoke. There is no uglier, more devastating smell. Still to this day, when I smell smoke, I am momentarily paralyzed.

I don't remember running to my apartment, but I was told I did. My first memory after smelling the smoke was standing on the corner, slowly realizing that my friends who were with me at the club were now standing next to me on the sidewalk. I remember seeing my car parked at a meter on the street, just as I had left it when life was normal and safe a few hours before.

My memory is so segmented. When I think back to that night, it feels like it was either a dream that I'm struggling to remember or like it didn't happen to me, like I'm remembering information told to me second-hand.

I remember seeing a woman screaming for help from her fifth-floor window. I remember a firefighter eventually rescuing her with a ladder. I remember the way the gray smoke hung in the air and the way the orange flames contrasted against the night sky. I remember wondering if I'd shut my balcony door so the smoke couldn't harm my two cats. I remember praying that the fire hadn't already gotten to them. I remember the panicked look on firefighters' faces as they rushed to save more people.

The five-story brick building looked like a huge monster, something too scary even for nightmares. It looked unrecognizable. I remember the chaos all around me—people screaming, first responders running, the entire block lit up by the lights of the firetrucks and ambulances.

Despite the chaos, I was calm. I said absolutely nothing. I retreated within myself, as I always do in scary situations. I pretend I'm not there. And then I pray that that's true.

Prayer. I can't even describe how much I prayed.

I was so naïve. I assumed the fire would be put out quickly. I assumed all the residents could get out safely. I assumed the only ones in real danger were pets, like mine, who needed to be rescued. Imagine my shock when I heard a woman screaming that her friend was trapped inside. I was dumb-struck. How could this happen? And then I heard about another person who was trapped. And another.

I remember my colleagues from the news station asking me for an interview. They knew I lived in the building and wanted to get my reaction. *My reaction?* I thought. *My reaction?* How can anyone accurately and articulately describe what it feels like when their world is burning down in front of them? My neighbors were in danger. I had no idea if my pets were safe. I was terrified. Even if I could form a sentence, I wouldn't have. I felt violated. It was in that moment I hated TV news and all it stood for. This was the first time I truly understood what it was like to be on the other side of the camera. For my job as a news photographer, I had filmed fires and other tragic events, and I had asked similar questions to the victims in those situations, but until that moment, until that gut-punch, I didn't truly know how it felt.

My next memory is of my parents pulling me away and helping me into a car where I left to endure the longest night of my life. I stared at a ceiling fan, unblinking, wondering what was left of my life. Helplessness is traumatizing. I'll never forget the feeling of knowing a tragedy was occurring, but there was absolutely nothing I could do about it.

I went back to the apartment as the sun was rising. Emergency crews were still on the scene. Even though the fire was out, they were still monitoring hot spots, and investigators were rummaging through the debris.

It was there that I learned nine of my neighbors died.

I told a first responder I had pets in my apartment, and much to my surprise, he allowed me accompany him inside to help find my apartment in the pitch-black building. Though the sun was shining on that brisk January morning, when we stepped through the front doors and into the foyer of the building, it was like walking into a cave. The smoke was so thick I remember thinking I'd suffocate. I could taste it. Water dripped from the ceiling. There were puddles on the steps as we walked to my apartment on the fourth floor. My hands were shaking as I fumbled for the key. The door swung open. The silence was sickening.

The Emmons apartment building was built in 1911. I loved it from the moment I saw it. My apartment had original hardwood floors and fireplaces, twelve-foot ceilings, elegant pocket doors in the large dining room, and built-in bookcases in the hallways. I worked two jobs to be able to afford rent, but it was worth it to live in a beautiful piece of history. In 1924, an adjacent apartment building was built, named Emmons Junior, and though the buildings shared a back wall, it was a fire wall, and that's what saved my building, Emmons Senior, from sustaining fire damage like Emmons Junior did. The fire started, and remained, in Emmons Junior.

My building had extensive smoke and water damage, though. The firefighter walked behind me as I called out for my cats, Claire and LeRoy. I didn't immediately panic when they didn't greet me because I knew they must be traumatized. When I walked into my bedroom, though, I saw LeRoy lying on his side in the floor. If I didn't know better, I would've thought he was sleeping. I saw Claire in my bed with her little face buried in the nightgown I'd taken off and tossed onto my pillow just before going to the comedy club the night before. They were gone, just like my sense of safety.

I retreated back within myself. I didn't say a word. The firefighter didn't, either. He took the pet carrier that I'd brought, thinking I'd be carrying living pets out of the building. Instead, it became their casket. When he moved LeRoy, I could see my fur baby's wet outline on the hardwood floor. That was the first time I cried. And I didn't stop for months after that.

When I walked back out in the sunlight, down the front steps of the building, there was the news crew again. They knew better than to ask me for an interview, but filmed me nonetheless. I watched myself on the news that night and saw tears streaming down my face, looking wide-eyed, scared, and unrecognizable, holding my pet carrier. I know my dad buried Claire and LeRoy under a rhododendron bush in his backyard, but I can't tell you if I was at the burial or not.

A few days after the fire, my neighbors and I were given one hour to grab as many of our belongings as possible before the building would be condemned and no one would be allowed inside ever again. There is nothing uglier than the aftermath of a fire. Soot-covered walls, broken windows, and cold, damp darkness will forever live in my nightmares. For days afterward, that scary-smelling smoke hung in the air; I smelled it wherever I went in town, and it felt like a black cloud hanging over my life.

I remember being at a local laundromat, washing the clothes I'd retrieved, and seeing the story about the fire on the national news.

I didn't know the people who lost their lives in the Emmons Junior, but my heart hurt for them anyway. I knew how it felt to lose pets to such a senseless tragedy, and I couldn't even begin to fathom what the victims' mothers, fathers, sisters, and brothers must've felt when they received the devastating news. It seems like it would be too much to process.

I will never know the extent of the pain the victims' families felt, but I went through my own emotions as a survivor of sorts. Every day, every single day, for months, I would wonder what would've happened if I hadn't gone out that night. What if I would've been home in a deep, deep sleep? I wondered why I was spared and those nine, innocent people had to suffer. I began to question God's purpose for my life and wrote about it in my journal for most of that year.

*I'm sitting here looking out the window of my new apartment wondering how I'm supposed to feel. I know everything happens for a reason. I know God had a plan for my life before I even had a life. But right now, in this moment, I don't understand what is happening to me.*

*Everything reminds me of that night. And everything I own smells like smoke. And to me, it doesn't just smell like smoke...it smells like my dead cats. And it's devastating. Completely devastating.*

*It is so weird. Looking back, it almost doesn't feel like I ever lived at the Emmons. I was beyond happy there. I know I was. But when I think about the Emmons now, I get this scared feeling, and it makes me wonder if I ever really enjoyed life there. I think I did, but my thoughts are so overlapped, and my mind is confused. I am so fragile right now. I question and re-question everything in life. Things come and go. People move. Animals die. Life is supposed to go on. But for me right now, I feel like I am at a standstill. And I'm too exhausted and too scared to move. I used to feel invincible.*

*I'm ashamed to say that now I am a crying, weeping, pathetic mess who can't be left alone. I (the girl who used to pride herself on being so independent) am afraid to be alone. It's so discouraging.*

*When tragedy happens, and the shortness of life is realized, it's hard to get motivated to try new things. I feel like, what's the point? I'm looking out of this window in my new apartment, ten stories up, seeing an incredible view, and I know I should feel blessed. I know I should realize how lucky I am to be sitting here with most of my belongings, smoke smell or not.*

*But I don't really feel lucky.*

*I cried myself to sleep last night over those cats. I slept with their toys, two rabbits—Claire's pink one and Lee's blue one. I put the cats' collars on the bunnies because I didn't have the heart to throw them away, but every time I hear the collars jingle, my mind is cruel: For a split second, I think Claire is getting ready to jump into bed. It's devastating when I realize I will never see her sweet face again. I feel like a bad cat mother. Could I have done something to save them? Surely, there must have been something I could've done, yet I did nothing and now they're gone. I have a lot of regrets.*

*Every time I hear a siren, I think of that night.*

*Sometimes I wake up in the middle of the night, terrified, with my hair matted to my tear-stained cheeks.*

*I try to think ahead to the future. I try to tell myself that one day life will be good, and one day it will feel right. It's weird how I don't feel safe anywhere. I think that's because I don't have a home. This new place isn't my home at all. I feel like I'm living in a hotel. It feels like punishment. I'm surviving, but I'm not happy. A major life change occurred, and I had no say-so in it; therefore, I feel cheated and confused and ill-prepared and angry and reluctant to move forward.*

*I don't know what the next move should be. I'm struggling to bounce back in a way I've never experienced.*

*If there's one thing I've realized, it's how important happiness is. Nothing is worth it if you're not happy.*

*Since the fire, when I think of the Emmons, I think of the scary hallway between the bedrooms where the ceiling is now falling in. I think of the darkness and how cold it is. I hope I don't always feel that way. That was my home. OOf all the places I've lived, that was my favorite, and it used to be my home. I think that's one reason it was so hard to leave that place yesterday. That, and also because it was the last place I lived with Claire and Lee. I hope I eventually remember no other place was more fun to decorate. No other place was as big. No other place had so much character. I loved my neighbors. I loved the atmosphere. I felt like I really lived my life there. I wrote, countless times, about how I felt like I was in the right place at the right time. It was such a beautiful building, and I pray I'm not in town when it gets torn down.*

*I know every experience in life makes me stronger. With that being said, I should come out of this year pretty damn tough.*

*I can see the world from this window. But right now, it belongs to everyone else when it used to belong to me. It seems so far away.*

*I just felt safe there. It's weird how deceiving life can be: the place I felt the safest turned out to be the deadliest. Now I question everything. I'm going to have to re-examine life.*

*And start over.*

And that's what I did—I battled daily tears and debilitating depression, questioning my existence like no young person should have to do, but I leaned on my faith, and because of that, I made it through that period of my life. I have no doubt I came through the darkness and found the light because of my trust in God. I rededicated myself to my faith at twenty-two years old, and that was the first time I realized how difficult, but necessary, it would be to rise above all the hurt and negativity in the world.

*I find it so hard to be a bright light in such a dark world. It's not hard because I want to do negative things; it's hard because I'm the outsider for being positive. If I told a random group of fifty college students two things: 1) I was going to preach about God in the middle of campus; or 2) I was going to pole dance tonight at Southern X, more people would be disturbed by the fact I was going to preach than if I would dance at a strip club. What is this world coming to? Christians are almost taboo now. When did religion become the thing to not do? It's sad: By the time I realized how much*

*I need God and faith in my life, I've become the outsider for following. The fire has really opened my eyes.*

*Here's how I feel everyday: I feel like, literally, I am on the outside of my life looking in. Know how I know? Because if someone asked me what drawer I keep my silverware in at my new apartment, I wouldn't be able to tell them. That's how I know. I'm so out of it that I don't know where the silverware drawer is. I couldn't tell you. That's how unaware I've become, and it's scary. In my mind, I still live at the Emmons. In my mind, especially in my dreams, my life is in apartment #19. I can see my birthday cake with white icing and multi-colored sprinkles in the fridge, the collection of dust in front of the sliding doors, the cat hair on the red rug, the open balcony doors with Lee's scratches on the base, the Cosmopolitan magazines on the coffee table, Mamaw's picture on the mantle, and the silverware in the fourth drawer from the top, laying on a black-and-white checkerboard placemat. A piece of me still lives at the Emmons. In my mind, Claire still sleeps on my hair every night. In my mind, I can still feel how soft her belly is. In my mind, I can still hear her purr. In my mind, I still have her.*

*Sometimes I even wonder if I have a grip on reality. It's not enough to experience tragedy…now I must lose my mind while I'm at it?*

*I definitely feel God calling me, but I'm not sure what He is saying. I'm not sure where to go or what to do. I want to help others. I want to help myself. I want to serve. I just need to be quiet and listen to God's directions.*

I hope I obeyed those directions. Perhaps I was being directed to live a more purposeful, intentional, Christian life. Or maybe writing this book to you now was what God was preparing me for all those years ago. Maybe passing down the lessons the tragedy taught me—about prayer, purpose, and conviction—to my children is my calling. I do believe that everyone is called, in some way, to be a beacon of light and hope in a world full of darkness and misery. I hope you act on whatever calling you think God has for your life.

Whenever I was haunted by the memory of the fire, you and Sissy were reminders that life would go on, and sunshine would lie ahead. You reminded me every day to be thankful. The fire taught me I cannot overlook or discredit the challenges I faced in my past because I knew I'd want to one day share what I learned.

I pray that you two never have to experience a situation like the fire. But I know this life is full of hurt, and you will experience your own version. I wish I could protect you from it. In fact, that's what keeps me up at night—knowing I can't save you from everything. It's that haunting feeling of helplessness all over again. Sometimes my fear suffocates me. My chest hurts. But I have to let you live and learn, just as I have.

My prayer for you is that you have prayers. And that you remember to pray. And that you remember someone is always listening and always cares. You have a purpose. Everything you encounter in life can be used as a learning opportunity if you choose to allow it to teach you. But it's not designed to be easy. I believe some moments in life are meant to be attention-grabbing. Maybe their intent is for you to retreat within yourself, examine your life, analyze the situation, and reemerge as a different version of yourself.

When the smoke clears, your faith will either be left to smolder...or it will be reignited.

# Nine

BILLY RUBIN COULD ALWAYS BE COUNTED ON FOR A laugh. Whether he was being intentionally funny, or just hilariously stumbling through life as kids (and adults) do, there was always something to laugh about.

Momma compiled a list of actual phrases she said to Billy over the years:

"Don't spit on the Play-Doh."

"Lizards don't eat Cheez-Its."

"Don't put mustard in your eyebrows."

"Get the diaper off your head."

"The dog doesn't want to kiss Mr. Potato Head."

"Don't lick the dump truck."

"Get that chalk out of your ear."

"I guess pizza doesn't float."

"No, we can't ride a pirate ship to school."

"Don't eat milk with a spoon."

"Get out of that bush."

"Don't hiss at the mailman."

"Say you're sorry for eating Sissy's eraser."

Some days, especially on those long, this-day-is-never-going-to-end, I-need-a-margarita-in-a-fishbowl kind of days, Momma often wondered why she had to say such phrases to any human, regardless the age. Most of this stuff seemed like common sense. But that's the awesome thing about kids—they don't have common sense, and they make you question yours. Billy taught Momma that on those long days when you feel like you're living in an alternate universe, it's best to just embrace the ridiculousness of it and succumb to the idea that lizards might like Cheez-Its.

And then laugh.

LIFE CAN GET HEAVY. SO IT'S IMPORTANT TO EMBRACE the moments in life that make us feel light.

I spend ten minutes every night slathering wrinkle cream around my eyes in an attempt to eliminate my laugh lines.

(Speaking of wrinkles, I have a joke for you: How many wrinkles does an asshole have? Smile, and I'll count them).

Just kidding, of course. I hope my salty language doesn't offend you. I've always been of the belief that a little salt is good for my diet. But I certainly don't want to displease those who choose to not season their vocabulary. A woman once told me I wasn't a "good Christian" because I dabbled in profanity. As if my positive attributes should be discounted because I enjoy the word "shit." I don't believe that's true. I don't think that when I'm standing at Heaven's pearly gates God will present me with a tally of the number of times I said a four-letter word.

Instead, I think He'd be more concerned about the judgment I cast upon others and my negativity toward them.

Here's how I see it: My sin may be different than yours, but we're all in the same imperfect boat. You can either smile and keep rowing. Or you can drown in your misconceived sense of superiority.

I choose to smile. And preferably, to laugh.

I was once contemplating getting Botox when I thought, *Why? Why am I trying to eliminate evidence of the hilarity in my life?* Laughter is such a beautiful thing.

Looking back on my life, I realize I spent the majority of my time laughing with (or at) you and Sissy. When it came to my "adult" world, things weren't, and still aren't, nearly as funny. And that's probably because errands, bills, and trips to the grocery store aren't a side-splitting good time. But I also think it's because adults have lost the ability to have fun and see the humor in things. They think way too highly of themselves. Dial it back, people. Everywhere I look—the news, social media, blogs—people are highly offended over anything and everything. They're angry. They're entitled. They're way too uptight. They're judgmental.

And that's usually when life bites us in the butt. I'll never forget my first outing with you when you were a newborn. I was taking myself way too seriously, trying to prove to myself, and the entire world, that I was the best mom ever. I dressed you, a tiny six-week-old, in khaki pants and an Oxford shirt and attached a pint-sized red bow tie. I then proceeded to take you to story time at Timrod Library. I had curled my hair and applied a face-full of makeup, and I sashayed into the building, probably with my nose in the air, trying to act like I had my life together.

Suddenly, I heard chuckling. People were staring at me. My ego assumed, at first, that they were smiling at you, my adorable son. They weren't. The entire time that I'd tried to paint the image of perfection, I'd been walking through the library with your vomit-covered bib Velcro'ed to my butt.

So there you have it, son. Life doesn't just bite you on the butt…it'll Velcro itself right to it.

Lesson learned.

And that brings me to my next lesson: Clothing is optional. Hear me out: One morning, as I was in a mad dash to get you and Sissy ready for school, you told me you wanted to pick out your own outfit and dress yourself. Choosing my battles, and deciding your wardrobe wasn't one of them, I agreed. You closed your bedroom door, and I could hear you rummaging through your closet. I was sure that my fashion sense had rubbed off on you and that you'd emerge looking dapper. I always wanted you and Sissy to dress nicely for school, and I was worried that if you weren't looking your best, other mothers would judge me.

Finally, the door opened, and you emerged, excitedly declaring that you were ready. You were wearing X-Men underwear (on backward), a Batman sock on your right foot, and a Santa hat. And that was it.

*Jesus, take the wheel.*

My first reaction was to be horrified. My second was to laugh hysterically. My third was to wonder how I could convince you to wear more clothing without crushing your excitement and without evoking judgment from the other parents. Then it hit me: *It doesn't matter what anyone else thinks.*

I convinced you to wear a Batman shirt to match your sock, and then suggested you put on the other sock to complete the look. You refused to wear jeans, but you did agree to wear Jetsons pajama pants. You wouldn't compromise on the Santa hat. It wasn't my ideal wardrobe choice for you, but you were happy, and I realized I was learning a valuable lesson in that (fashionable) clothing is optional. I did still worry that other moms would think I was crazy, but I decided I needed to be as confident in your decision as you were. I was too uptight. There, I said it. Self-honesty equals freedom, and perfection is boring. Seeking validation only invalidates me.

Reveling in this newfound confidence, I turned to my journal to vent my frustrations about the uptight people of the world.

*To the woman parked next to me at the red light today: I see you, lady. I see the judgment in your eyes and the disapproving frown on your face as you watch me crush the drum solo in the song "Wipe Out" using makeshift drum sticks— my hairbrush in my left hand and a half-chewed lollipop (thanks, Billy) in my right. I see you. And you know what I think? I think you could use a few more drum solos in your life. Bless your heart.*

Billy, do you know what else uptight people need? Old-person dance class. That's right. They have not lived until they've watched an eighty-seven-year-old booty-pop. If that doesn't bitch-slap the frown right off their pompous pouts, I don't know what will.

I love old-person dance class. I go three times a week at my local gym. It's technically a Zumba fitness class, but to cater to the clientele (the majority of whom are sixty-five and older), the instructor plays a lot of 1950s-era rock-n-roll. The gals and I love doing the monkey to "Rockin' Robin." We're like watching an army of robots that have short-circuited.

But it's not all oldies music. There's one rap song in which the artist insists, "If you're sexy and you know it, say 'Oh yeah!'" And the ladies, all twelve of us, scream, "Oh, yeah!"

I started attending these dance classes when you were in preschool, and back then, as a woman in my early thirties, I was timid. I didn't scream nearly as loud as my counterparts in scenarios like the rap song. I still had somewhat of a hang-up about what other people thought of me. I made it my goal to work on it, but that sense of freedom came with age.

Take Mrs. Rose for example. Years ago, after completing my first dance class, I came home and immediately wrote about her in my journal.

*She can only dance with her right leg, because her left knee is stiff with arthritis, and she leans on a cane. But she whips that cane around like a lasso, and yells, "Get it, girl!" Sometimes, she accidently farts, which is unfortunate because I'm usually standing behind her. But you know what? She. Doesn't. Give. A. Shit. How awesome is that? If I farted in*

*front of someone, I would be red-faced and mortified. But
not Mrs. Rose. I need that freedom and confidence in my own
life. I have a feeling I'm going to learn so much more than
dance in this class.*

And I did. Now, as a woman nearly as old as Mrs. Rose was
back then, I am grateful for everything dance has taught me,
but I still have my struggles. For example, last week, at the end
of class, the instructor turned on Shakira's "Africa" and insisted
we improv to the African beat.

I will never forget the lyrics; they were words of encour-
agement belting out over the speakers.

*The pressure's on,
You feel it.
You've got it all,
Believe it.*

Despite my age, I consider myself a somewhat skilled danc-
er when it comes to a technical routine that I can practice and
perfect. But to have to stray from a routine and come up with
something random in the moment terrifies me, even though I've
worked very hard throughout the years to overcome my fears by
stepping out of my comfort zone. My therapist says there are two
types of people in this world: People who bend like flowy trees,
and people who are stiff like rigid trees. I'm a rigid tree. I want
to be a flowy tree, much like ones found here in the Lowcountry
covered in wispy Spanish moss, but instead, I'm like one of those

dead, decaying Palmetto trees at Botany Bay. Remember that eroded beach we used to visit? You called it a "boneyard of trees" along the shoreline. While they're certainly beautiful in their own right, those suckers won't be sprouting new leaves any time soon. There's no growth. To be the best version of myself, the healthiest version, I need to grow and change at every stage of my life. I've learned that life is too fluid to have rigid expectations.

As "Africa" continued to blast from the speakers, I went for it.

*Listen to your God,*
*This is our motto.*
*Your time to shine, don't wait in line,*
*Y vamos por todo.*

I know nothing about African-inspired dancing, and I'm quite sure I looked like a fool, but I hopped on one foot, turning in a circle, waving my arms above my head.

*People are raising their expectations,*
*Go on and feed them.*
*This is your moment,*
*No hesitations.*

I threw my head back. I shook my hips. I smiled ear to ear. You know what? It felt great to let loose.

*Today's your day,*
*I feel it.*

*You paved the way,*
*Believe it.*

That's what it boils down to: believing in yourself. Giving yourself validation and not waiting around for others to do it. You *are* good enough. You *are* brave enough. You *are* strong enough. You are *enough*.

I couldn't wait to record this moment in my journal.

*I thumped my cane against the floor in rhythm with my freedom and my newfound confidence. I thumped it in memory of Mrs. Rose and all she taught me. I felt so happy. My cheeks hurt from smiling so much. For the first time, probably in my entire life, I didn't care what anyone thought of me. This was my dance. I owned it. And I looked around the room at the other women owning it. We were all from different walks of life, in different stages of that life, and were sharing something very empowering. I noticed how beautiful each woman's dance was. I'm ashamed to admit that there was probably a time when I would've laughed at Mrs. Edith, who was wearing just a sports bra and yoga pants, doing hip thrusts. But you know what? You can't laugh at someone who is already laughing. She beat the rest of the world to the punch. So we are left to laugh with her. A happy soul is contagious.*

Those women are strong, confident, and funny. And as a result, they're happy. I've watched my life come full circle on that dance floor. Once a naïve thirty-something held back by my fears and laughing at the old lady who farts in class, I'm now the old lady breaking wind and breaking down boundaries. I am doing things I never thought I could do, and I hope I can be an inspiration to someone the way Mrs. Rose was to me.

My prayer for you is that you never take yourself too seriously; that you always see the beauty in a new dance; that you aren't afraid to take chance; and that if you're sexy, and you know it, say "Oh yeah!"

# Ten

BILLY RUBIN IS KNOWN FOR HIS HAIRSTYLE. HE WAS the only kid in preschool to get his hair cut by a stylist at a non-kid salon. He didn't sit in a chair resembling an airplane, and he didn't wear a cape with cartoon characters on it. Instead, he went to Momma's salon where all the women drooled over him. They said he looked like a politician in his sweater vest with his hair parted to one side, slightly tousled with gel. And he had been getting his blonde combover perfectly styled since he was three months old. Haircuts were serious business in Billy's house.

Funny side note: For years, Billy believed the act of brushing his hair gave his locks fragrance, like that of washing with shampoo. Every morning, he'd waltz into Momma's bathroom, grab her hairbrush and use it to swoop his coif to the side. When finished, he'd confidently ask if his hair "smelled yummy" before strutting out of the room.

When Billy turned three years old, he became a rebellious "threenager." He no longer listened to instructions or minded his manners. He was bossy, nonsensical, and unreasonable. Even the most common of tasks couldn't be performed without a dramatic scene.

Billy was on a roll. Momma was on anxiety medication.

During what seemed like his one-thousandth trip to the hair salon, Billy forgot how to act. Instead of sitting still, he stole the stylist's comb, pretended it was a microphone, and jammed out to the song "Wild Thing."

(Billy grew up listening to songs from Momma's generation. When she'd take him to school in the morning, she told him the only radio station her fourteen-year-old Toyota Camry could pick up was the "oldies" station, so Billy learned to love the Rolling Stones, Led Zeppelin, and, of course, Van Morrison. In reality, Momma was lying about the Camry's inability to get other stations; she simply didn't want to hear a protest from the backseat when she tuned in to her selection).

Momma warned Billy that if he didn't hold still, the stylist would accidently buzz too much hair with the clippers.

*Wild thing, you make my heart sing.*

Her first warning was ignored.

*You make everything groovy, wild thing.*

Her second warning was ignored.

*Wild thing, I think I love you! But I want to know for sure—*

Before Momma could even issue the third warning, an ill-timed head roll by Billy distracted the stylist, and the clippers accidently swiped a chunk of hair right off the top of his head.

Instead of looking like a cool Wild Thing, he looked like a crazed character from the book *Where the Wild Things Are*.

Momma was wide-eyed and silent, not knowing whether to be mad or sad. Billy stared down at the patch of hair in his lap and burst into tears. He'd clearly decided to be sad.

The stylist had no choice but to buzz his entire head, instead of just the sides as she normally did. It took two months for his combover to grow back. And during those sixty days, every time Billy looked in the mirror, it was a reminder that actions have consequences. While it was shocking at first, it was actually one of the greatest things to happen to a threenager; it was physical proof that you can't act like a fool and expect to go unscathed.

Also during those sixty days, Billy slowly returned to his happy, agreeable, if not ornery, self. One night, Momma asked Billy if he had learned his lesson at the salon. Billy hugged her, and while in Momma's arms, he finally got to finish the words to the song he started six weeks prior:

*Come on and hold me tight. You move me!*

AS I WROTE IN THE LAST CHAPTER, SOMETIMES LAUGHter is essential to get through the challenging moments. But it's also important to remember, in those moments, a serious lesson: Actions always have consequences.

It'd be easy to write a chapter regarding actions and consequences pertaining to children. I think as adults, it's harder to admit that, one, we make mistakes, and two, those actions have consequences. We tend to believe that because we're adults, rules don't apply to us.

In my life, one of my most challenging yet most rewarding experiences has been my marriage. Marriage is hard. Really hard. There are all sorts of hurdles from small ones like adjusting to how annoyingly he gargles mouth wash to big ones like how my anal-retentive behavior affects him. It's a constant give and take; a constant choosing of the battles. Marriage is one big compromise. And it's remembering that my feelings are not the only ones involved and realizing that he, in fact, has feelings. It's about learning to put another adult first. It's easier for parents to put our children's wants and needs before our own. But when it comes to our spouse, we get selfish. Putting two adults, who are opposites in many ways, under one roof and telling them to form a healthy, productive life together is hard. And then throw some kids into the mix and this thing called marriage becomes even more challenging. I'm constantly reminding myself that it's okay he forgets stuff, just like I hope he's reminding himself it's okay that I only cook the same five meals every week. (Spaghetti, again?!). I also have to remember it's okay to argue, but it's not okay to hit below the belt. It's okay to disagree, as long as we have a civil discussion afterward. We've been together almost forty years, and I still need to remember it's okay that we're not always on the same page at the same time. Marriage is about bending toward the other person. It's about being present and available. It's about thinking as a team instead of as individuals. It's about accepting that our actions have consequences.

It sounds cliché, but marriage is a journey. It's not just about two people journeying through life together but also about the journey of becoming two people who can peddle through life in sync.

For our fifth wedding anniversary, your daddy and I went back to St. Simons Island. We left you and Sissy with Farfar.

After driving the three hours from our home in South Carolina to St. Simons, we decided to stretch our legs by renting a quadricycle.

A quadricycle is a four-wheeled bicycle-car complete with two steering wheels, two seats in the front and two in the back, and a canopy roof. It even had headlights.

Made entirely of steel, the quadricycle wasn't as easy to peddle as one might think. Graff and I were definitely burning our glutes while burning the rubber. We peddled out of the rental shop's parking lot, discussing which direction to go. Of course, I wanted to go right, and your dad wanted to go left. He compromised and turned right. There was a steering wheel in front of me, in the passenger seat, but it was non-functioning. So I was compromising, too, by trusting Graff to guide us. I slowly learned it's okay to occasionally give up control.

During the first phase of our journey, the bike path took us beside the ocean. The wind was blowing across the dunes; the air was warm and salty. A yellow butterfly flew alongside us. Graff and I were so excited, having never ridden a contraption like that before. The newness was invigorating.

The sun bounced off the gray-blue water of the Atlantic. We passed teenagers grilling hotdogs and playing volleyball. We waved to other bicyclists on the trail. We saw a beautiful resort and promised ourselves we'd stay there during our next trip to the island.

We arrived at a stop sign, and Graff made his left-hand turn. The excitement in my gut that had momentarily died down was back again as we ventured into the unknown for the second phase of our adventure. We peddled through the

Island's village, passing a charming antique store and Zuzu's diner. Shaded by trees covered in Spanish moss, this trek was refreshing; the air was cooler, and it finally felt like October after what seemed like an unrelenting and scorching summer.

We crossed the street, leaving the shadowy village and were immediately blinded by sunlight. The final phase was along the marsh. The smell of pluff mud shot straight to my brain. It smelled like home. Reinvigorated for this final leg of the trip, I took in the beauty around me: pelicans wading through the shallow marsh, a boy and his grandfather fishing from the pier, and the view of the St. Simons Island Lighthouse in the distance.

In what felt like the blink of an eye, the journey was over. And as we returned the quadricycle to the rental shop, it occurred to me that our three-part journey that afternoon could represent our three-part journey in life: the first part was pre-children; the second part includes the years we spent parenting you and Sissy; and the third would be Graff and I as empty-nesters.

Now that we're in the third stage, it truly does feel like it all happened in the blink of an eye.

The other day, a fuzzy memory invaded my brain. It was of Mamaw and her last moments in her hospital bed. I kissed her. Told her I loved her. The doctor confirmed she was gone. And I died a little, too. I wondered how I would do life without my safe person. Suddenly, there was a knock at the hospital room's door. It was Graff, my then-boyfriend, coming for a surprise visit. My mouth hung open, my eyes welled with tears, and my heart exploded with understanding and gratitude: Mamaw had sent me a new safe person. And I'll be forever grateful that I've gotten to peddle through life with him.

Thinking back on our quadricycle trip, it would've been impossible to do alone. To peddle that huge vehicle definitely required a team effort. There were times when my legs were tired, and Graff would offer to do all the pumping, and vice versa when he needed to rest, but for the most part, we did it together.

And that's the gist of marriage.

Throughout the three phases, we encountered obstacles and celebrated victories. There were times we were excited about the journey and times we were restless. But we persisted, together, and when we reached the end, we were thankful for the experience.

And that's the gist of navigating life with your partner.

Your daddy keeps this quote in his wallet: "The perfect marriage is just two imperfect people who refuse to give up on each other."

Speaking of not giving up, during that five-year anniversary trip, Graff and I went back to the pier where he threw our message in a bottle into the ocean. Holding hands, we carefully balanced on slippery rocks as we navigated downward toward the shoreline. The tide was out, unlike it had been the night he'd thrown the bottle. The eternal optimist in me hoped we'd find the bottle half buried, stuck between some rocks, ready to be rescued by us. Thousands of tiny crabs scurried along the damp sand as our eyes darted from rock to rock. We spent an hour searching, and as the tide crept back in, we decided we would eventually find our message, but not that day.

Back at the Village Inn, where we were staying, I jotted down my thoughts.

*I think it's fitting that we didn't find the bottle today. Its journey is not over, just as ours is not. I do wish, though, that I could remember what the poem said. I remember parts of what I wrote, but not the poem in its entirety. I guess it'll just make it that much more special when we eventually find it.*

*I was so entranced while searching the rocks that I didn't even noticed how far we had walked. When I looked up, we were at the lighthouse, at the stairs that descend into the water at high tide. I remember writing in my journal there, while sitting in the lighthouse's gazebo, when Graff and I were just dating. In the blink of an eye, nearly ten years have passed, two people have become one, and two new lives have been created. I'm glad we have this place to come back to so we can remember us at our foundation. I'm so glad we're here.*

The rest of that trip was also memorable: The first night, your daddy drank too much whiskey and fell asleep, on top of the bedspread, still wearing his sport coat. The second night, cruising the island in a golf cart, the cart broke down in the middle of a thunderstorm, and Graff and I were soaked down to our underwear. On the third night, we went to bed at 6 p.m.

Like our quadricycle ride, those experiences are a meta-phor for marriage (and life): Sometimes you're down and out; sometimes you're out and wet; and sometimes you're out cold. Meaning, you'll get knocked down, either by self-sabotage, poor timing, or necessity, but when the sun rises the next day, so do you and your partner; growing together (meaning, simul-taneously) and growing together (meaning, in conjunction).

And that's my prayer for you. I pray you can always grow with your partner; may your journey always be enjoyable, meaningful, and challenging. As partners, I hope you two re-alize that hitting cruise control is boring and hand-holding during the rough terrain is essential. I hope you appreciate the value of off-roading, Wild Thing.

# Eleven

BILLY RUBIN LOVED ANIMALS. THE FIRST TIME HE WENT to the zoo, he only said one phrase the entire day: "Oh! Look at that, Momma! That's my favorite!"

Every animal was his favorite.

But his "very most favoritist" was a kangaroo. When Momma was pregnant with Sissy Bobo, Billy thought Sissy was a baby kangaroo who lived in Momma's pouch. (He was very disappointed when she was born and didn't have fur).

Every time he left a zoo, his elation was always overshadowed, though, by his fear that the kangaroos weren't getting enough to eat. He always volunteered to feed them, but was disappointed when the zoo attendant handed him what appeared to be lettuce. He reluctantly shoved his little fist, full of the leafy vegetable, through the fence and offered it to his furry friends.

Billy thought it was salad. Billy hated salad and figured the kangaroos did, too.

During a subsequent trip to the zoo, Billy couldn't get to the kangaroo exhibit fast enough. He even bypassed some of his other interests—the elephants, the zebras, and even the monkeys (Momma's favorite).

Once at the kangaroos' home, Momma noticed Billy's bulging pockets in his shorts, but she wasn't fast enough to stop him from pulling out what he thought was a better alternative to salad: ravioli.

Yes, ravioli.

He'd taken his leftovers from dinner the night before to feed the kangaroos. They nearly caused a stampede, scrambling to get to him. They licked his hands, his arms, his shirt. One kangaroo stood up, leaned over the gate and licked him right in the face, its tongue raking upward, taking Billy's hair up with it.

Billy looked pretty pleased with himself. Momma was looking around nervously to see if any zoo attendants had witnessed the ravioli roundup.

She then noticed Billy reaching into his other pocket attempting to offer the kangaroos a second course, but she was able to stop him before he shared his other favorite foods: Cheetos, Skittles, and cheesecake.

Momma was left to clean up two messes: the pockets of Billy's stained shorts and his hurt feelings. He really wanted to feed the kangaroos what he thought was a yummy meal. After Momma explained how much kangaroos actually like the lettuce, Billy realized there were other ways he could help his "very most favoritist" animals. He broke out into song (The Beatles' "I Want to Hold Your Hand"), singing the marsupials bedtime music so they could more easily take a nap.

Billy's sweet spirit always had him thinking about others. He especially wanted to help those who couldn't help themselves. He decided his next project would be to feed his sister ravioli, Cheetos, Skittles, and cheesecake because he was still convinced she was a furless kangaroo.

Helping others can be just as challenging as accepting that our actions have consequences, perhaps because we're too oblivious to realize when people are in need or because we don't know how to help or because it's easier to look the other way than to lend a hand.

People ask me why I still work so much at my age. And there's a very good reason: I enjoy helping teenagers.

When a new client comes into my office, I'm reminded of how teenagers desperately need help, not only in the form of educational guidance, but also regarding compassion. I love working with this age group because of their excitement for life; their naivety is charming and their ambition is honorable. But in some cases, know-it-all attitudes can give teenagers a bad rap. I encounter my fair share of teens like this—they either don't listen to advice, lie about progress, or pretend to have all the answers. But I try to remember to have patience, grace, and understanding for these young people who are trying to navigate life and figure out their place in it.

Being a teenager is hard. (Don't pretend like you don't remember. And don't pretend like you were a perfect angel). Behind their arrogant attitudes, there lies true vulnerability and fear. And it is our job, as adults, to look beyond the façade and determine what is making these kids put up a wall in the first place. Then, we must work to break it down, all the while, loving them through the chaos.

It's easy to look at teenagers today and think their only concerns in life are where to shop, who to Snapchat, and what to order at Starbucks. But I know better.

I'll never forget proof-reading the college admission essay of a shy, timid seventeen-year-old girl. When asked to describe her biggest challenge to date, she wrote about her brother who had just been killed in a car accident and how she was struggling to adjust to life without him. Or the essay of a student who was unapologetically brazen: She had just confided in her parents that she was gay. Or the essay of a boy who never completed his assignments: He'd just found out his brother had cancer. Or the essay of the girl who seemed mad at the world: Her father never returned home from a tour in Afghanistan. As the saying goes, you can't judge a book by its cover; the pages contain hurt, sadness, uncertainty, and insecurity that may never be depicted at face value. Some kids hide from their realities, some overcompensate for their insecurities, some are lost in their emotions, and some lash out. There's no right way to handle a difficult situation, for a child or an adult. These are human beings, and they don't need judgment, resentment, or negativity. They need our help.

Not every teen, or adult for that matter, is going through a tragedy. But everyone has struggles. It's much easier to walk away than to invest the time or energy needed to help. I believe that's why so many people choose to look the other way when someone is in need.

I'm reminded of the parable of the Good Samaritan in Luke 10:25. In this scripture, Jesus is asked what one must do to inherit eternal life, and the answer is "to love the Lord your God with all your heart and with all your soul and with all your strength and with all your mind, and to love your neighbor as yourself."

When asked for clarification on who, exactly, constitutes as a "neighbor," Jesus tells this parable: "A man was going down from Jerusalem to Jericho, when he was attacked by robbers. They stripped him of his clothes, beat him and went away, leaving him half dead. A priest happened to be going down the same road, and when he saw the man, he passed by on the other side. So too, a Levite, when he came to the place and saw him, passed by on the other side. But a Samaritan, as he traveled, came where the man was; and when he saw him, he took pity on him. He went to him and bandaged his wounds, pouring on oil and wine. Then he put the man on his own donkey, brought him to an inn and took care of him. The next day he took out two denarii and gave them to the innkeeper. 'Look after him,' he said, 'and when I return, I will reimburse you for any extra expense you may have.'"

Jesus then confirmed that of the three, the one who behaved like a neighbor was the one who showed mercy.

Loving your neighbor as yourself is so important that it's described as one of God's most important commandments. But as with other ways we should show neighbors we love them, such as acceptance and forgiveness, helping them is difficult to do. It's much easier said than done. It's also very easy to pretend like we don't understand the meaning of the word "neighbor" by choosing to take it literally. Jesus doesn't just want us to treat those who live next door to us kindly and with mercy; we must treat everyone we encounter with that same grace. And that's hard to do because even if we don't want to admit it, we don't feel like everyone we encounter deserves our love. This world we're living has a "me, me, me" mentality, and the stench of arrogance and selfishness.

Loving your neighbor isn't an isolated event. You can't just perform a kind act once and consider the task completed. That's another reason this commandment is so challenging. It's not one incident; it's a lifestyle.

On the evening of June 17, 2015, when nine members of Emanuel African Methodist Episcopal Church in Charleston were murdered by a white supremacist after a Bible study, the world stopped here in South Carolina for us, as you well know. The victims, ranging in age from twenty-six to eighty-seven, welcomed the gunman, a stranger, into their church to worship with them before he opened fire. Three members of Mother Emanuel, as the church was affectionately called (because it is the oldest AME church in the south), survived the shooting. Authorities determined it was a racially-motivated attack; the gunman specifically targeted the church, whose members are predominantly black.

I remember your daddy waking me up early the next morning, shoving his phone, with a news article explaining the carnage, in my face. As my eyes adjusted to the screen, and my brain struggled to comprehend what I was reading, I remember feeling confusion about how something so evil could happen in a place of peace. How could someone be filled with so much hate? How could someone have complete disregard for the lives of human beings? How could someone be so offended by the differences of others?

There was some beauty to come from the ugliness, though. I remember how the community came together to support not only the survivors, but complete strangers. People from all different religions, cultures, ethnicities, and races showed their love for their neighbors. Characteristics that perhaps might've once divided them didn't matter anymore. People were living like disciples. They were showing mercy and compassion, love and kindness, grace and support. They were loving their neighbor as themselves. It's a shame that in today's world it takes a horrific tragedy to shock people into decency.

I'm glad I recorded my perspective of the next few days in my journal because it's refreshing to read about in a world currently experiencing so much hate.

*The shooting is on the front page of every newspaper; the steps of Mother Emanuel are awash with flowers and candles. Locals aren't the only ones standing arm-in-arm on the sidewalk outside of the church praying—people from all over the country, even all over the world, have come to show their support. Parents are bringing their kids, teaching them to hug a crying stranger and to bow their heads to pray with them.*

*Everywhere I go, I see "Charleston Strong" on banners, murals, and decals. I drove behind a car today with the South*

*Carolina state tree—the Palmetto—depicted on a decal on the back window, with nine doves where the palm leaves would be, one dove flying upward, indicating the rest would follow up to Heaven.*

*People from all walks of life held hands to span the two and a half miles across the Arthur Ravenel Bridge overlooking Charleston. To see miles of people holding onto one another forming one cohesive unit was astounding. I will never forget the aerial photos I saw on the news tonight. Police estimated about fifteen thousand people showed up to pay their respects and show their solidarity. They may have been from different walks of life, but in that moment, they were all representing the hope and beauty we will see with eternal life, when our time here on earth is finished.*

*The most incredible moment, though, in my opinion, was learning about the mercy shown by a victim's grieving family member. I read that when given the chance to address the shooter during a bond hearing, the victim's relative told him she forgave him and would pray for him. Even as she described the excruciating pain of losing her loved one, she told the shooter he was forgiven.*

As the days went on, and the shock subsided, I witnessed people slowly returning to their old ways. They'd come together in grief only to then be divided again once their memories of the tragedy faded. How quickly people forget the pain of others but hang on to their own grievances. This issue is not limited to South Carolina; it's a worldwide dilemma. People go back to hating different cultures and races, thinking it takes a strong person to stand up against those they dislike or with whom they disagree. What they fail to realize, though, is that it takes a far braver person to love neighbors than it does to hate them. It takes a stronger person to show mercy to someone he doesn't like and to then change his perspective regarding why he disliked that person in the first place. It's easy to hate; the world is full of it. I hope you understand that to love is to be at peace with yourself and your own life; to love is to realize the differences of others do not and cannot affect you unless you let them; and to love is to realize that you are loved and forgiven, therefore, you should do the same for others. You may think they don't deserve it. But you know what? Neither do you (yet you're loved and forgiven anyway).

When I think about the relative of the Mother Emanuel victim, who forgave the shooter just days after he took her loved one's life, I get emotional. That was a powerful moment the world needed to see. And that was a powerful act on her part because forgiveness can be hard.

Every night, when your daddy and I pray together, there's a special phrase we say that I once heard from a pastor:

*Take us where you want us to go.*
*Show us who you want us to meet.*
*Tell us what you want us to say.*
*And keep us out of your way.*

As disciples, it is our job to go where God calls us to go and do what He calls us to do. In addition to helping and loving my neighbor, He also wants me to forgive. And that can be hard for me.

Not forgiving is selfish and self-destructive, especially because each night during prayer I ask God to forgive me. I know that I've reached my height when I'm on my knees, asking for forgiveness. But it doesn't end there. I must also be willing to do the same for others.

I'm reminded of the parable of the unforgiving servant in Matthew 18:21. The disciple Peter had asked Jesus how many times he must forgive his brother when he sinned against him. Jesus uses the parable to illustrate that Peter, the rest of the disciples, and every Christian, must forgive an infinite number of times.

In the parable, a servant owed the king such a large sum of money that the debt could never be repaid. In jail, the servant admitted his debt and begged the king for forgiveness. The king felt compassion for the servant and released the debt. Once released, the servant encountered a friend who owed him a small debt, and instead of forgiving the debt as his debt had been forgiven, the servant attacked his friend and demanded the payment. The friend then ironically found himself in the same situation the servant was in, but was shown no mercy. The king punishes the servant for not showing his friend the same kindness.

The king's willingness to forgive such a large debt perhaps illustrates God's forgiveness of our sins, and the servant's refusal to release his friend's debt illustrates someone who does not appreciate his or her own forgiveness. I do appreciate my forgiveness, but I know I don't always act like it.

I think it's because I assume forgiving means forgetting. If someone hurts me, my refusal to forgive them is my attempt to protect myself from future pain. Or I assume that telling someone they are forgiven means I'm giving that person permission to hurt me again. Neither are true.

Refusing to forgive doesn't hurt anyone but me. It doesn't punish the other person or teach them a lesson. It only robs me of my happiness. Forgiveness actually means loving myself enough to not let the weight of carrying a grudge destroy me.

The concept of forgiveness was truly an epiphany in my life. Seriously. It hit me like a lightning bolt while driving one day. I was thinking about the grudges I had been holding, and the hurt I felt, and then I thought, *Who am I to not forgive?* God forgives me of my sins over and over and over again. It goes back to unconditional love. I continually screw up, and He continually forgives me. So who am I to not forgive others? It was on that day I chose to forgive, accept, and change my expectations.

I once read that there are three ways to undoubtedly fail at life: First, complain about everything. Second, never be grateful. Finally, blame others for your problems. I agree with those three, but would add a fourth: the inability to forgive.

The first prayer I learned to recite as a child was the Lord's Prayer. But the issue with reciting it was that it then became too routine. I'd say it so often that I wouldn't really hear the words and comprehend their meaning.

*Forgive us our trespasses as we forgive those who trespass against us.*

There it is, in one of the most spoken prayers on the planet. It's written in Matthew 6:9 that this is not only how we are supposed to pray, but how we are supposed to live. Yet any number of factors—my stubbornness, my ego, my ignorance—all prohibit me from forgiving as I am called to do. Sometimes I catch myself thinking, *Well, I can't help how I feel.* But that's not true. If I'm feeling negatively, it's because I am allowing myself to feel that way. I am in control of the thoughts inside of me and the words that come out of me. I am in control of allowing myself to forgive and asking for forgiveness for myself. No excuses. No blame-shifting. The ability to forgive has proven critical in my life. I realized I cannot advance in life with a peaceful soul and a clean conscience if I cannot let go of past transgressions.

Here's another phrase (told to me by a pastor) that helps me when I need a reminder as to why forgiveness is so important: "The costs are high; the time is now; the way is forward."

I'll be honest (and pray he forgives me): I don't remember what his sermon was about. I remember loving the phrase and writing it down, but looking back, I can't remember what, exactly, it pertained to. But then I realized it could pertain to many, many things, one of them being forgiveness. The cost of not forgiving is high—too high. The time to forgive and release that burden is now. And once you are free of the load, you can move forward. I can't promise forgiving will mend a broken relationship—that would require forgiveness and understanding on the part of the person who hurt you. And you can't control that. But what I can promise is the undeniable peace you will feel afterward.

Before you are able to effectively help others, you must be able to forgive them. If you can't, your actions are empty. Helping and forgiving go hand-in-hand. Just as the "Charleston Strong" supporters joined hands to span the Ravenel Bridge, mankind must also stand in solidarity by forgiving and helping.

My prayer for you is that you realize it's never too late: Never too late to lend a hand; never too late to forgive; never too late to love your neighbor as yourself. Always remember that words matter, and oftentimes, those who spew the harshest words are the people who need to hear kindness the most.

When I was pregnant with you, a friend stitched a proverb on a small, yellow pillow for your nursery and gave it to me at my baby shower. It read, "God couldn't be everywhere, so He created mothers."

I believe God created a special maternal guardian in Mother Emanuel, perhaps to demonstrate to the world that love and forgiveness are attributes of the (Charleston) strong.

# Twelve

ON BILLY RUBIN'S SECOND BIRTHDAY, HE RECEIVED several gifts: a new swing set in the backyard, a pirate costume, and a basketball hoop. But Momma hoped his favorite gift, the one he'd remember forever, was the surprise she told him about at the end of his birthday party: He was going to be a big brother.

He said his favorite was the pirate costume.

He refused to discuss the baby business. When Momma brought up the subject, he'd walk away in protest. Two long weeks after hearing the news, Billy finally looked pitifully up at Momma and asked, "Why a baby?"

Momma explained that babies were a wonderful gift from God, and that they should say a prayer to thank Him.

Billy refused to bow his head and pray.

So then Momma explained that Billy would be getting a baby sister, and sisters are super fun. Billy could dress her like a pirate; he could push her on his new swing set; and he could teach her to shoot hoops.

Billy told Momma to buy his sister her own toys (meaning, he wasn't sharing his).

After many failed attempts at discussing his baby sister, Momma gave up and decided Billy would talk about her when he was ready. That day came when Momma was seven months pregnant, and the impending change was inevitable.

Billy skipped happily over to Momma, rubbed her round tummy, and with a big smile on his face, he declared he wanted to help Momma with his baby sister when she arrived.

Elated, Momma asked what tasks Billy wanted to tackle.

"I want to wipe her butt," he exclaimed.

"You want to wipe her butt?"

"Yeah!"

Momma didn't know how to respond. At first, she wanted to say, "Learn to wipe your own butt first, and then we'll talk." But she didn't. She didn't want to shutter this newfound communication regarding the baby.

For the remaining two months of Momma's pregnancy, Billy looked forward to cleaning poopy diapers (if only Momma could've been that happy about it). Momma did, however, demonstrate to Billy the other tasks he could help with, such as picking out pajamas, brushing the baby's hair, and feeding her a bottle. But Billy was all about the butt-wiping.

When the time finally came to meet his sister at the hospital, as fate would have it, she had a dirty diaper. But when the cloth was pulled back and the mess inside was revealed, Billy decided his role would no longer be "butt-wiper" but instead, "wipe-retriever," as he'd fetch the wipes and hand them to Momma so she could clean the nastiness.

Billy may not have realized it in the moment, but he was given a special gift in his sister. He gained not just a sibling,

but a life-long friend— someone he learned to love unconditionally while receiving unconditional love in return. He
especially loved Sissy when he dressed her in an eye patch
and pirate hat.

UNCONDITIONAL LOVE. IT IS DEMONSTRATED WHEN A
person has the ability to forgive the transgressions of others
and love his neighbor as himself.

Then there's the unconditional love a mother instantly
feels for her child, the minute he or she is born.

I believe that's the way God loves us.

One of my most cherished memories with you and Sissy
is when we participated in the Living Christmas Story at our
church. Every year, a few weeks before Christmas, we would
dress in costumes and partake in an event which depicts Jesus'
parents, Mary and Joseph, and their journey to Bethlehem
where Jesus was born. Even now, more than two hundred
volunteers come together every evening for this three-night
event. People from all over the state of South Carolina visit,
eager to drive their cars through the church's parking lots,
which are transformed into scenes replicating the holy journey: a bustling market filled with treasures such as brass,
jewelry, and fabrics; an angel on the mount surrounded by
a field full of live donkeys, sheep and goats; a pottery wheel
and blacksmith's shop; the inn where Mary and Joseph were
told there was no room for them; and of course, the manger
where Jesus was born.

Over the years, I've volunteered for numerous roles, mainly ones that demonstrate my stellar acting abilities, such as a shepherd (it's a non-speaking role, and I simply pet the sheep).

One year, though, I got my big break. I was asked to portray Mary. True, I was asked to be Mary because there were no other infants available other than you to play the role of baby Jesus. But I took the job seriously, and like any seasoned actress, I practiced for this starring role.

On the night of the performance, your daddy, who was playing Joseph, and I, wrapped you in the white swaddling blankets, laid you in the manger, and waited for guests to arrive. As our scene began, actors portraying the Three Wise Men brought gifts over to you, but instead of looking at you lovingly, they looked horrified. One of them mumbled under his breath, "Check the bottoms of your sandals; I think someone stepped in donkey crap."

In my heart, though, I knew it wasn't the donkey. You were supposed to be portraying the King of Kings, but you had just taken a royal dump in the manger.

End scene.

I was shocked when Graff and I were asked to play Mary and Joseph again, three years later, when Sissy was a baby. I remember looking down at her, lying on the hay, swaddled in the white cloth (sans poop). She stared up at me with wide, sky-blue eyes, and I thought, *Why a baby?* I wanted to know why God sent His son into our world to save it, but He chose to send Jesus as a baby. That doesn't seem very powerful; in that moment, Sissy looked so fragile, helpless, and innocent, I can only imagine people in Jesus' time being dumbstruck when they realized the future ruler of the world would come to them as an infant. God had the ability to send Jesus to us in any form, at any age, with any number of powers. But He chose a baby. Why?

Perhaps it's because being a baby made Jesus relatable. It made him seem like he's one of us, even though Jesus is fully human and fully divine, simultaneously. Infancy is a sign of humanity. It's the true definition of love. No matter how many times you've witnessed a birth, it's awe-inspiring and humbling. It's a gut-check.

Also, I believe it's easier to follow in the footsteps Jesus took as a man after knowing he crawled as a baby. He came into this world just as you and I do, facing the same challenges and temptations, taking on the human journey.

Additionally, it's important to note that Jesus entered the world in an unnoticed way, and in an unnoticed place, to unnoticed people. For example, shepherds witnessed his birth—people who often felt unloved and unappreciated. That's how God usually comes to me (and probably to you)—in unassuming places and by unusual circumstances when I need Him the most.

Life is filled with such circumstances—many of them difficult. But a baby represents hope and new beginnings. When I was pregnant with you, people told me there is no greater love than that between a parent and a child. It is unconditional, and unapologetically so. It's the only way we as humans can even begin to fathom how much God loves us.

Parenthood is purposeful. It's more than leading your child through life; it's leading your child to life.

I'm going to give you perhaps the most important parenting advice I ever received: As a Christian, it's not enough to lead your children to Jesus; you must bring Jesus to them. In Mark 5:35, Jairus, a synagogue leader, is devastated by the death of his daughter. He went to Jesus, asking Jesus to come to his house. Once there, Jesus heard the crying and said, "Why all this commotion and wailing? The child is not dead but asleep."

People laughed at him.

Jesus took the girl by the hand and told her to get up. Immediately, she stood and began walking. Everyone was astonished. Before leaving, Jesus told those who witnessed this to not tell anyone, and then he instructed the girl's parents to give her something to eat.

*Give her something to eat.* What you feed your children is important. Faith should definitely be on the menu. Love and hope also nourish the soul. That story illustrates the importance of bringing Jesus to your children, but don't just call upon him when a miracle is needed. True, he's definitely good for those. But it's important to invite him in to be a part of their everyday lives. I tried my best to do that with you and Sissy.

One night, after we said our prayers, and thanked God for our blessings (you thanked Him for toilets), you said you wanted Sissy to sleep in your bed. I kissed you two good night and closed the door. Forever your safe person (whether you realized it or not), I sat on the stairs and listened.

I heard you tell Sissy, "Close your eyes; I'll be right here if you need me."

I cried. I was such a sap. The love you had for each other made me love you two even more, and I didn't think that was possible. I wrote in my journal until I fell asleep.

*I'm listening to my greatest blessings hug each other as they fall asleep, which reminds me how sweet life truly is. I face hurdles every day, and think the problems are bigger than they actually are, but knowing my children are resting peacefully confirms that nothing else matters but them, our love, and this life we have together. Truly, I thank God every day for making the four of us a family. Graff and I were total strangers who found each other against the odds, and together, we created this family that I love so much I can't even put it into words. I don't feel worthy of these blessings; I am not deserving. But despite that, God's unconditional love for me allowed me to, in turn, show unconditional love to these three special people. Out of everyone in the world, these three are mine. I feel immensely grateful, fiercely protective, and undeniably humbled. I hope Billy and Sissy always know that no matter what, I'll love them. No matter what. I hope they grow to become people they're proud of. They never have to worry about me feeling pride because I always will. I hope they feel the freedom to find themselves, the confidence to create their own lives, and the security of knowing I will always be behind them.*

And as much as I always wanted to remain steadfast in my desire to allow my kids to grow up and determine their own identities, I need to acknowledge that it's one of the hardest lessons to learn as a parent, in my opinion—my kids aren't me, and that's okay. You and Sissy are individuals. And neither of you has to be like me. When you were a child, my job was to love you, nurture you, feed and clothe you, protect you, and shelter you (literally and metaphorically) until you were old enough to do those things on you own. But that's where my hands-on role stopped. Now that you're adults, I cannot make you have my beliefs, and I cannot tell you how to behave, think, or feel. I don't have that right. Even though I birthed you, and raised you, you are your own people. Everyone is free to create their own identity. And truly, that's what I ultimately always wanted as a parent—to raise independent, self-sufficient individuals who are steadfast in their beliefs (whatever they may be).

This rule doesn't just apply to people with kids. All adults have the right to choose their own path. No one should feel guilted into being like his or her parents. A person can be just as smart, just as successful, just as funny, just as talented charting his own course. A parent's path isn't the only road worth traveling.

On nearly a daily basis, all throughout your childhood, you'd say to me, "I can do it by myself." I knew, of course, that you couldn't do everything on your own. And as your mom, it was really hard for me to let go, knowing you might fall. In the early years, the falling is literal. As you got older, it was met-aphorical. In both circumstances, though, it scared me. But I always tried to remember that falling was essential.

For your third birthday party, we invited no fewer than thirty preschoolers to join in on the fun. Two hours into the party, frantically searching for a glass of wine, I ventured out-side to survey the scene. I immediately stepped in a puddle of vomit on the sidewalk, the result of someone consuming co-pious amounts of sugar. I then looked up and saw a kid asleep on the front lawn. Two empty juice boxes lay beside him. A few feet away, more empty juice boxes were strewn about. Three boys were chasing each other in their underwear, their shirts tied around their heads like bandanas, their pants MIA. A Power Wheels Jeep had been crashed into the refreshments table and was missing a door; the disfigured birthday cake had been karate-chopped by a guest; and a kid (who wasn't on the guest list) was rubbing the remaining icing across his upper lip creating a blue mustache.

Replace the juice boxes with beer bottles, and it could've been a scene from my college days.

And if I think about it, preschoolers and young adults have two things in common: They're trying to find themselves, and they're making a lot of mistakes while doing it. It was so hard for me, as a parent, and as someone who made similar mistakes, to step aside and let you make them, too (not that having fun at your birthday party was a mistake; although, you did learn some valuable lessons, like don't stick the lollipop up your nose. And God knows you made a lot of mistakes in college. *No judgment, though*).

When you were growing up, I, of course, had an obligation to keep you safe. As a young child, you had poor judgment, minimal self-control, and you lacked life experience (as all children do). But to some degree, I have to constantly remind myself that even though I will always have more life experience than you, it doesn't mean you don't have valuable insight. I don't want to one day have a fifty-year-old son who I am constantly judging because I, his seventy-nine-year-old mother, have more life experience than him.

I don't want to do that to you because I know how it feels from the other side. I was met with opposition, and what I assumed was judgment, when making several choices in my life—changing careers, moving away from my hometown, how I would parent my children, just to name a few. It's hard for parents to make the transition from being the mother/father of children to the mother/father of adults. (Yes, they will always be children in the sense that their mother birthed them, but they will not always be adolescent-aged and need parenting, and it's important for parents to remember that.)

I'm sure what my loved ones were ultimately feeling was concern; they care about me and didn't want me to make a mistake. What I once viewed as judgment or disagreement, I now realize was fear. I may not have always realized it at the time, but my parents unconditionally loved me and always wanted the best for me (even if our definitions of what was best clashed). They were scared of me making what they viewed as a bad choice. I always felt loved, supported, and encouraged when I was making decisions they agreed with, but not so much when I was going against the grain. And that's understandable—it's hard for parents to love, support, and encourage through times of strong opposition, even if they want to. I have found myself encountering that same struggle as a mother of adult children, and I've had to remind myself several times that you're not being disrespectful by disagreeing with me or by choosing to do something different than I would've chosen—those situations are all about you meeting yourself. It's you realizing who you are and embracing and exercising what you believe.

I also want to remember that my job isn't to prevent you and Sissy from making mistakes or encountering obstacles—and I can't face the hardships for you. My job is, and always was, to hold your hands through the chaos and help you up if you fall. But to completely shield you wouldn't have helped you become self-sufficient adults who can handle adversity and challenges.

I remember often worrying that I was making a "wrong" decision when I chose to do something different than anything I'd witnessed growing up. Our instinct as humans can be to mimic the actions and behaviors we've seen from people we idolize, like our parents. But I slowly came to realize that my decision was not wrong if it was right for me.

Parents will always struggle with the need to protect their children. I know I'm far from perfect. When you find me over-stepping my bounds, I hope you will remember three things: One, I want to earn forgiveness when I mess up (and I don't expect to be automatically forgiven simply because I am your mother. The fact that I birthed you doesn't give me a pass to treat you unfairly); secondly, I truly want to be what you need; and finally, regardless of what you do in life, I will always love you unconditionally.

I know it sounds cliché, but we only have this one life. One life. That's it. And we have no idea how long or short it will be. If we spend the majority of that life feeling miserable, then another trip around the sun hardly seems enticing. We have the right and the responsibility to make a change. But no one can do it for us. We can't whine about circumstances we refuse to adjust, and we can't start the process of altering if we aren't willing to put in all the hard work required. What I learned is that I owe it to myself, your daddy, and you kids to be the happiest version of myself I could be. Was I, or am I, happy all the time? Heck no. But I know I strive every day to be the best version of myself: the happy version. And in turn, happiness breeds happiness. I always wanted you to grow up in a world knowing change is okay and happiness is a choice. And I continue to want to be strong enough to accept that you're going to make your own choices and create your own happiness, far different than anything I could probably ever imagine for you. And I also want, and need, to support your choices. Accepting and supporting are two different things. You and Sissy deserve both.

I've found in my sixty trips around the sun that, the majority of the time, people who can't accept change or support ideals different from their own are either scared of upheaval or unhappy with their own lives. Or both. And instead of getting mad at the people in our lives who don't support us, we need to see that those people don't need our anger; they need our compassion and support (even though we're not receiving that support in return).

I will end this chapter with a note I wrote to you (but never gave you) after an argument we had when you were seventeen. You'd gone to sleep with a candle burning on your dresser, and it caught the book next to it on fire. Luckily, your daddy was passing by your room at the exact right moment and was able to extinguish the flame. But I grounded you for a month because all I could think about was the Emmons tragedy. The thought of losing you was as suffocating as the smoke billowing from your room. You told me you thought I hated you, but in reality, I'd never been more aware of the depth of my love for you. I wrote the note in an attempt to explain my love despite your anger toward me and my frustration toward you, and above all else, I wanted you to know that even though you made a mistake, one that left me crying for three days, I still believed you were becoming one of the most remarkable men I'd ever known.

*Even though I'm upset with you in this moment, when I think of you, I think of happiness and love. I always have. And I always will. When you were younger, nothing made you happier than to dress like a pirate (and force Sissy to wear an eye patch and be your "matey"). Do you remember that happiness? That doesn't even come close to describing how happy I am to be your mother.*

*The moment you were born, a mother was born. With both you and Sissy, I loved you from the very moment I realized I was pregnant. I yearned to hear your heartbeats and cried happy tears every time I saw you in an ultrasound. There are no words to describe the moment of your births when the doctor placed each baby on my chest. Both of you latched onto my index finger, and I never wanted you to let go. Time stood still, and life would never, ever be the same.*

*If there was such a thing as consciousness in the womb, I would hope that while there, you felt content, warm, and safe, surrounded by the presence of everyone who loves you. I believe that's what Heaven will be like. And that's why our bond, sweet Billy, is so strong. God always has a plan: A baby is never born without a mother. Though not every mother or every situation is ideal, we bring you into this world, and I have never taken my job to guide you through life lightly. I have never been a perfect parent, but I have tried to lead to the best of my abilities, and it has been my life's greatest pleasure.*

*Just as God had a plan for our arrival into this life, He has a plan for our departure. Of course, I do not know when mine will be, but I promise you, I will spend my every breath thanking Him for you. I will never be able to whisper enough thank-you's to express my gratitude, but I will continue to try. Just as I will try to be the very best me for the very deserving you. There are times when I question my maternal abilities, but I have never questioned my love for you. And I hope you don't either. If I've taught you nothing else in this life, I hope you've learned that forgiveness breeds peace, peace breeds acceptance, and acceptance breeds love. I hope you always remember that there's true beauty in the differences of others, that bravery is required to chart your own course, and that you cannot go to sleep until you get down on your knees, every single night, and thank God for your blessings, both large and small. Above all else, I hope you understand the meaning of unconditional love. That's the love I have for you. That's the way I feel every time you belly-laugh and every time you cry; every time you hug me and every time you slam your bedroom door in my face; every time you thank me and every time you take me for granted; every time you succeed and every time you sit the bench. I love you. And if you can fathom that type of love, I will have done my job, because that's the type of love God has for us, His children. We don't always earn it, and we rarely deserve it, but we are unconditionally loved. I hope you go into this world, and show that same type of love to others. That is my prayer for you.*

# Epilogue

STARING IN THE HALLWAY MIRROR, I'M REALIZING THAT what I just did was every bit as gut-wrenching as I anticipated it being.

I readjust my blonde wig, catching a glimpse of my mauve nails as my gold bangles slide from my frail wrist up toward my boney elbow.

Telling you that I've been undergoing chemotherapy to combat breast cancer was almost as difficult for me to say as it was for you to hear. Now that you've left, I'm pulling myself together, making sure my false eyelashes aren't lopsided, and replaying our conversation in my head.

The most important thing I wanted you to realize is that this is not a death sentence. I can't die yet; I still have things to meet, most notably my first grandchild, Van Morrison, and my goal of retiring to St. Simons Island. In many ways, I feel like I've only recently met myself, therefore, it simply cannot be time to meet my maker.

When I move to St. Simons, I want to buy a little cottage near the lighthouse. Maybe I'll name it *Two Buoys and a Gull*, since I'll be living there with your daddy and Hollie Jr. Maybe

I'll name it *Born Before the Wind*. I definitely will not name it *Conch Out*, though, because, while clever, that's not my plan. I still have a lot of life to live.

*Seas the Day*, perhaps?

Speaking of the island, a wonderful thing happened to me while writing this book for you. As I was reading through my old journals, trying to decide what to include in this project, I found a fragile, yellowed piece of paper stuck between some pages. It was the rough draft of the poem I wrote for your dad—the message we put in our bottle. We spent many, many hours looking for that bottle throughout the years, thinking its discovery would be our only hope of unlocking the past and revealing the long-forgotten message inside. In reality, it had been with us the entire time—as was our faith and love.

*Our tale is a special one.*
*Romeo and Juliet, prepare to be outdone.*
*After searching a sea of fish, I drew a heart in the sand,*
*And fell in love on St. Simons Island.*

*We were a perfect match, though we lived miles apart.*
*So I asked God for patience and to mend my lonely heart.*
*Months turned into years. Winter turned into spring.*
*You finally moved near me. And then came the ring.*

*A girlfriend became a fiancé. A fiancé, a wife.*
*We bought our first home and settled into life.*

Whispering "sweet nothings" became a thing of the past.
Now we fussed over whose turn it was to take out the trash.

The trick to making a relationship work isn't that hard.
It's about finding joy in little things, like working together
in the yard.
So we worked, laughed and played. We kissed and made some
lovin',
And the next big excitement was a bun in the oven.

Our baby was a miracle, a gift from above.
And to think it all started with some puppy love.
A family was created, so I asked God for all the right answers.
He said, "You learn from your mistakes. Just keep saying
your prayers."

Months turned into years. Winter turned into spring.
We taught them to ride bikes and then gave them wings.
Our kids grew up and flew away. It was just us again.
So I thanked God for the ride and asked for some grandchildren.

Our family grew in numbers, though it started with just
two.
Now wrinkled and gray, you were still the most handsome
man I knew.
What a journey we were on—side by side, hand in hand.
And if I had the choice, I'd do it all over again.

*I found that what I suspected in the beginning was actually
a fact:
Best friends can become lovers. And opposites do attract.
Something else that I've realized time and time again,
Is that God always provides sunshine after the rain.*

*Near the end of the journey, I reflected on my life,
Wondering if I was a good mother, and if I was a loving wife.
I held your hand as we climbed Heaven's stairs,
Remembering all of my "wifely" prayers.*

*You told me you'd always felt loved. Then what you said next
reassures,
While I had been saying my prayers, you realized I was the
answer to yours.
God had given me everything I'd ever wanted, and it was
nothing I deserved;
Strength, patience, guidance…many lessons learned.*

It was like I wrote that poem at the end of my days, not the beginning. Being able to read those forgotten words showed me that God granted the desires of my heart. However, the gifts were not instantaneous, and sometimes, they even felt torturous… and I think that's by design. Because being granted my desires doesn't mean my life was free of undesirable circumstances. Again, this life was never intended to be free of pain. And truly, thinking back on my experiences, I wouldn't have wanted it to be. All situations are learning opportunities (and those painful ones are the best teachers), and while I was busy trying to be a teacher to my children, you were actually the ones doing most of the schooling.

Even now, I find myself enlightened by my unborn grandson—New life inspires new hope. I believe my cancer battle is an undesirable situation—a blip, really—in the life I always prayed for. He's a reminder to count my blessings rather than my burdens and to always be grateful (for both).

I realize God uses children to teach adults what they need to know; children demonstrate the beauty and grace in this life, and they have the uncanny ability to keep our intended journeys interesting. If you think about it, God and children possess the same remarkable qualities; they are faithful, kind, and merciful. And both provide an accurate reflection—a true mirror—of our souls.

The last line of the poem reads:

*I thanked God for our life, feeling truly blessed.*
*Then He took our hands and said, "I have something to confess."*
*"I am a fisher of men, and what I'd always planned,"*
*"Was for you to find love on St. Simons Island."*

When my first love and I buy our cottage on our island, I've decided I will name it *Salt and Light*. As Christians, God calls us to be the salt of the earth and the light of the world—basic, fundamental goodness and beacons of hope.

I *hope* you'll find a little salt and light in this book, sweet Billy. Embrace its message as you embrace your first-born. I pray he always feels content, warm, and safe; may he be someone who seeks the light and is never afraid to come out of his shell.

Raise your glass, and his bottle, to this remarkable time of transition. Cheers to his first cicada summer.

51550765R00093

Made in the USA
Columbia, SC
19 February 2019